KNOWN
UNKNOWNS

KNOWN UNKNOWNS

100 CONTEMPORARY TEXTS TO COMMON TUNES
JOHN L. BELL & GRAHAM MAULE

Wild Goose Publications
Wild Goose Resource Group

First published 2018

ISBN 978-1-84952-567-1
Text, cover image & design
© 2018 Wild Goose Resource Group,
c/o Iona Community, Glasgow G5 9JP, Scotland.
www.wildgoose.scot

John L. Bell & Graham Maule/ Wild Goose Resource Group
have asserted their rights
under the Copyright, Designs & Patents Act 1988,
to be identified as the authors of this work.

Published by Wild Goose Publications,
Glasgow G5 9JP, Scotland.
www.ionabooks.com

Wild Goose Publications is the publishing division
of the Iona Community.
Scottish Charity No. SC003794.
Limited Company Reg. No. SC096243.

The Wild Goose is a Celtic symbol of the Holy Spirit.

All rights reserved.
No part of this publication may be reproduced in any form
or by any means, including photocopying
or any information storage or retrieval system,
without written permission from the publishers.

A catalogue record of this book is available
from the British Library.

Printed by Bell & Bain, Thornliebank, Glasgow

MIX
Paper | Supporting
responsible forestry
FSC® C007785

**To
Ian Fraser
in his
101st Year**

Contents

13 **Introduction**

14 **The Songs**

Number Title (for First Lines see Index on page 128)

1. God's Intended Joy
2. Ageless God
3. All The Wonder
4. All Who Throng The Halls Of Heaven
5. Among Us And Before Us
6. And Did You Know?
7. Easter Evening
8. Because The Saviour Prayed
9. Because You Had An Upstairs Room Prepared
10. Bless, O My Soul
11. Christ Has Risen
12. Come, Host Of Heaven
13. Conceiver Of Both Heaven And Earth
14. Do Not Be Vexed
15. For All The Saints
16. For Each Time There Is A Season
17. From Adam Came The Apple
18. From Heaven's Attendant Host You Came
19. Give Us, This Year
20. Go, Silent Friend
21. God And Parent Of All People
22. God Beyond Glory
23. God, Give Us Life
24. God It Was
25. God Loved The World So Much
26. God Our Creator
27. God's Is A World Of Beauty
28. God's Spirit Came At Pentecost
29. God's Spirit Is Here

Contents

30. Help Us Accept The Past
31. How Can We Stand Together?
32. I Come In Faith And Fear To God
33. I Love The Lord
34. I Owe My Lord A Morning Song
35. The Beggar
36. I Waited Patiently For God
37. Inspired By Love And Anger
38. Fellow Travellers
39. Jesus Calls Us
40. Jesus Christ Is Risen
41. Jesus Christ Is Waiting
42. Jesus Was Doubted
43. Just As A Lost And Thirsty Deer
44. Keep Me, Lord
45. Let Every Nation On The Earth
46. Long Have You Loved Me
47. Lord Jesus Christ, Shall I Stand Still?
48. Lord, When Your Kingdom Comes
49. Monarch And Maker
50. No Wind At The Window
51. The Pedigree
52. Not Through Merit
53. O Christ, You Wept
54. O God, With Holy Righteousness
55. O God, You Are My God Alone
56. O Lord, Our Lord
57. The Web Of Love
58. Oh Where Are You Going?
59. Out Of The Direst Depths
60. Praise The Lord, The Ground Of Goodness
61. World Without End
62. Praise With Joy
63. Shout For Joy
64. Sing, My Soul
65. Sing Praise To God
66. Sing To God With Joy And Gladness

67. Sisters And Brothers, With One Voice
68. The Day Soon Will Come
69. The God Of All Eternity
70. The Hope That Hides In Bethlehem
71. The House Of God
72. The Love Of God Comes Close
73. The 'Other Person'
74. The Innocents
75. The Time Has Come
76. The Whole Creation Waits
77. The Word Of God Is Like A Lamp
78. There Is A Line Of Women
79. The First Miracle
80. This Is God's House
81. Though Hope Desert My Heart
82. Through Abraham And Moses
83. We Cannot Measure
84. We Come, Dear Lord, To Celebrate
85. We Did Not Know
86. We Do Not Ask
87. We Rejoice To Be God's Chosen
88. For Those Whose Song Is Silent
89. The Hand Of Heaven
90. God On Earth
91. When God Created Humankind
92. When Joseph Was Bridegroom
93. Gifts Of The Spirit
94. The Truth That Sets Us Free
95. Torn In Two
96. God's Surprise
97. The Summons
98. With Grace And Carefulness
99. Within The Circle Of Your Friends
100. Women And Men As God Intended

Indices:

- 127 **Copyright**
- 128 **Alphabetical Index of First Lines**
- 132 **Common Tunes & Their Metres**
- 135 **Psalms In Paraphrase**
- 136 **Subjects & Themes**
- 138 **Wild Goose Resource Group**
- 139 **Wild Goose Resource Group Titles**

Introduction

We are hoping that the phrase 'Known Unknowns' is not copyright, and that if it were, a former USA Secretary of State is not so impoverished as to claim royalties. But we thank him for an apt description of the contents of this book.

None of the tunes suggested have music notation provided. They are the kind of tunes which most people with some familiarity with church and folk music should know.

The unknown factor is the texts. Some have appeared before in our previous publications to known tunes, some to dedicated original tunes. But almost fifty per cent have never appeared in a hymnal or song book. As with all our songs, none were written for publication; they were written for people and only after being sung in different places and amended through kindly criticism, did we feel able to share them more widely.

The texts represent a gamut of subject matter, everything from paraphrases of psalms to songs about ecology, child abuse, money, depression and delight. And they are put together here especially for the kind of churches we particularly want to encourage – churches where there is no musician, churches where there is a reluctance to sing new songs; churches where the praise of God has been kept separate from the concerns of the world.

Songs appear in alphabetical order and are followed by an index of tunes and of subject matter. The vast majority of the tunes can be found in any hymnal, and frequently two will be suggested for a text. The subject index should be helpful when looking for songs to suit a particular theme in the readings or liturgy.

We dedicate this book to the Revd Dr Ian Fraser who, in the

Introduction

nineteen sixties helped to stoke the fires of what became known as the 'Hymn Explosion'. In company with the hymnologist Eric Routley, Ian invited potential tune and text writers to come to Scottish Churches' House in Dunblane and develop their craft in company with each other. Few of the products from these gatherings remain in publication, but what was in effect a 'hymn laboratory' encouraged and inspired writing on both sides of the Atlantic.

Ian is now in his hundred and first year and he still has time for writing. Long may that continue.

Finally, we'd like to thank Sandra Kramer, Jo Love and Gail Ullrich for their immaculately diligent proofing.

John L. Bell
Graham Maule
The Wild Goose Resource Group
Epiphany 2018

The Songs

Holy Scripture / Joy / Saints of God
Kingsfold 8686 D (DCM)

1

GOD'S INTENDED JOY

1. Aged ninety and a hundred years,
   our ancestors were told
   to bring a child into the world
   despite their being old.
   So Sarah giggled, Abraham laughed,
   and when they birthed a boy
   they called him Laughter as a sign
   that God's intent is joy.

2. Much later, Miriam beat the drum
   when safely on dry land;
   and David danced before the Lord
   that all might understand
   how fears dispelled and hopes restored
   are gifts without alloy,
   all meant to celebrate the truth
   that God's intent is joy.

3. So Jesus at the wedding feast,
   when all had drunk their wine,
   replenished empty glasses as
   a kindly gift and sign
   that happiness and deep delight
   are meant, in heaven's employ,
   to show a dour and doubting world
   that God's intent is joy.

4. Not shallow, precious sentiment
   or forced frivolity;
   not novelties to entertain
   or fabricated glee;
   but deep as lakes and bright as light
   which nothing can destroy,
   and meant for every human heart
   is God's intended joy.

JLB

Creation / Truth
Holy Manna 8787 D

AGELESS GOD

1. Ageless God of boundless wonder,
   endless source of peerless grace
   who, to shatter speculation,
   came incarnate face to face;
   you we praise, almighty Maker,
   parent of humanity,
   power behind the powers we cherish,
   Lord of life as life should be.

2. None among us stood attentive
   when you brought the world to birth;
   nor can any claim full knowledge
   of the future states of earth.
   Fascinated, still we struggle
   to make sense of what has been,
   and with differing dreams imagine
   what, as yet, remains unseen.

3. Each idea still gestating,
   each conviction in its youth,
   each encounter, each engagement,
   each impassioned search for truth –
   these we offer, not for blessing
   but for shaping to your will.
   Here, good Lord, inspire, amaze us,
   fire our insight, fuse our skill.

4. Train our science to be servant
   of the needs we must perceive;
   teach our intellects, where blinded,
   that to see we must believe;
   in our politics prevent us
   from confusing means and ends;
   and through faith and doubt direct us
   to pursue what Christ intends.

JLB

3   *Creation / God's Grace*
Ar Hyd Y Nos   8484 8884

ALL THE WONDER

1. All the wonder that surrounds us
   springs from God's care:
   all that marvels or confounds us,
   raw, rich or rare;
   touch and texture, sights and voices,
   nature's countless forms and choices,
   all in which the heart rejoices
   springs from God's care.

2. Every creature, every human
   lives by God's grace:
   every family, man and woman,
   culture and race;
   those whom fortune seems to favour,
   those exploited for their labour,
   those who need to know a neighbour
   live by God's grace.

3. How can we revere God's goodness
   meant for all time?
   How ensure that each uniqueness
   keeps in its prime?
   How can we revere with pleasure
   all God gives for life and leisure?
   How preserve each earthly treasure
   meant for all time?

4. God has willed that peace and justice
   walk hand in hand.
   These, with love, shall build foundations
   on which we'll stand:
   love for lover, friend and stranger,
   love defying death and danger,
   love as firstborn in a manger –
   heaven close at hand.

JLB

4   *Creation / God's Majesty / Praise of God*
Ebenezer (Ton-Y Botel)   8787 D

ALL WHO THRONG THE HALLS OF HEAVEN

1. All who throng the halls of heaven
   praise God's awesomeness and power;
   unseen angels, bowed in worship,
   sanctify each sacred hour.
   God's voice thunders over waters,
   fathoms oceans, stirs the sea,
   full, majestic, measured, mighty,
   glorious through eternity.

2. This same voice can split the cedars,
   towering trees of Lebanon;
   and demand that solid mountains
   skip and scurry on and on.
   Sound and sight are intermingled:
   God's voice flashes like a fire;
   desert places writhe and tremble
   rumbled by the Lord's desire.

3. God's voice sets the forests quaking:
   leaves are stripped and treetops stare.
   Though earth trembles, heaven rejoices:
   'Glory' echoes everywhere.
   Over flood, untouched by chaos,
   God, alone enthroned, is king.
   May God's peace and heaven's blessing
   anchor us and everything.

Paraphrase of Psalm 29

5 *Holy Communion / Jesus' Life & Ministry*
Sursum Corda 10 10 10 10

AMONG US AND BEFORE US

1. Among us and before us, Lord, you stand
   with arms outstretched and bread and wine at hand;
   confronting those unworthy of a crumb,
   you ask that to your table we should come.

2. Who would say No, when such is your resolve:
   our worst to witness, suffer and absolve,
   our best to raise in lives by God forgiven,
   our souls to fill on earth with food from heaven?

3. Who would say No, when such is your intent
   to love the selves we famish and resent,
   to cradle our uncertainties and fear,
   to kindle hope as you, in faith, draw near?

4. Who would say No, when such is your request
   that each around your table should be guest,
   that here the ancient words should live as new,
   'Take eat and drink – all this is meant for you'?

5. No more we hesitate and wonder why;
   no more we stand indifferent, scared or shy.
   Your invitation leads us to say Yes,
   to meet you where you nourish, heal and bless.

JLB & GM

6   *Holy Communion / Lent & Passiontide*
Eventide 10 10 10 10

AND DID YOU KNOW?

1. And did you know, that on the very night
on which you washed your own disciples' feet,
one whom you loved would leave the upstairs room
and scurry through the dark to price your head?

2. And did you know that those you trusted most,
who tried your patience and enjoyed your love,
who knew your fondest stories off by heart
would soon desert you in the dead of night?

3. And did you know that while it yet was dark
your fiercest enemies would rub their hands,
and scoundrels who were game for any bribe
would lie and lie again to seal your fate?

4. Did you know this when, with your healing hands,
you broke the bread and shared the cup of wine,
and feasted in the face of certain death
that we in this place may do so again?

5. Then, Jesus, on your fearless faith we lean.
Here let us taste the food and drink of heaven,
and in it own the brokenness we cause,
and through it know that all can be forgiven.

This text is especially appropriate for use on Maundy Thursday

JLB

7   *Easter*
Eisenach / Conditor Alme Siderum   8888 (LM)

EASTER EVENING

1. As we walked home at close of day,
   a stranger joined us on our way.
   He heard us speak of one who'd gone,
   and when we stopped he carried on.

2. 'Why wander further without light?
   Please stay with us this troubled night.
   We've shared the truth of how we feel
   and now would like to share a meal.'

3. We sat to eat our simple spread,
   then watched the stranger take the bread;
   and, as he said the blessing prayer,
   we sensed a greater presence there.

4. No stranger he; it was our eyes
   which failed to see, in stranger's guise,
   the Lord who, risen from the dead,
   met us when ready to be fed.

5. Alleluia! Alleluia!
   Alleluia! Alleluia!
   As Mary and our sisters said,
   the Lord is risen from the dead!

JLB & GM

Christian Unity / Lent & Passiontide
Woodlands 10 10 10 10

BECAUSE THE SAVIOUR PRAYED

1. Because the Saviour prayed, 'May they be one',
and taught his friends to say, 'Your will be done',
we own our need to live by God's own Word
and walk together following Christ our Lord.

2. Our narrow loyalties have had their day –
these separate paths evading Jesus' way.
We sadly own the scars that mar the past
yet gladly seek the road God made to last.

3. We are our Saviour's body: Christ the head,
first born of God, first risen from the dead.
Competing, we debase his holy will;
engaging, his intention we fulfil.

4. So, guide us, Lord, and take us by the hand,
and show us how to love and understand;
reveal, within the differences we share,
the pattern of your glory, grace and care.

5. And when our journey here has reached its end,
and strangers are the pilgrims you intend,
may we as one, forgiving and forgiven,
enjoy you in the harmony of heaven.

JLB

9

Holy Communion / Lent & Passiontide
Sursum Corda   10 10 10 10

BECAUSE YOU HAD AN UPSTAIRS ROOM PREPARED

1. Because you had an upstairs room prepared
   and set aside a special place and time
   in which to share a sacred meal with friends,
   so we reserve this place and time for you.

2. Because you took a basin and a towel
   and stooped to wash the feet of those you loved,
   so we think not of what we have to give
   but of your wish to love and serve us here.

3. Because you blessed the produce of the soil,
   and said that bread and wine would be your host,
   so we believe that as we keep this feast
   you'll keep your promise and be here again.

4. Because you broke the bread and shared the cup
   to symbolise your sacrifice for all,
   so we let go of all we covet most,
   and lean on you and yearn to be made whole.

   (Communion may here be shared)

5. Because you told your friends, 'I give you peace,
   a peace the world can never own or end,'
   we leave this table keen to reconcile
   and, though diverse, to show that we are one.

6. Thanks be to you, our Saviour, for this feast,
   and for our place in your community.
   Take us from here to follow where you call,
   together bound in justice and in joy.

JLB

10   God's Grace / Praise of God
Richmond 8686 (CM)

BLESS, O MY SOUL

1. Bless, O my soul, bless God the Lord,
   the one from whom you came;
   let all within me be stirred up
   to bless God's holy name.

2. Bless, O my soul, the Lord your God,
   and never once forget
   the many gracious benefits
   God gave and gives you yet.

3. Pardon for all the wrong you've done,
   healing from every ill,
   rescue from ruin and from death –
   these spring from God's good will.

4. God's love and mercy crown your life;
   God meets your deep desires;
   the Lord, who makes the eagle soar,
   your new-found life inspires.

5. Bless God, you mighty angel throngs
   fulfilling heaven's command;
   bless God, all you attendant hosts
   who serve at God's right hand.

6. O bless the Lord, in heaven and earth,
   you creatures of God's word;
   and you, my soul, stir up yourself
   to bless and worship God.

Paraphrase of Psalm 103 (abbreviated)

JLB & GM

11

Easter
Blaenwern / Hyfrydol   8787 D

CHRIST HAS RISEN

1. Christ has risen while earth slumbers,
   Christ has risen where hope died
   as he said and as he promised,
   as we doubted and denied.
   Let the moon embrace the blessing,
   let the sun sustain the cheer,
   let the world confirm the rumour:
   Christ is risen! God is here!

2. Christ has risen for the people
   whom he died, through love, to save;
   Christ has risen for the women
   bringing flowers to grace his grave.
   Christ has risen for disciples
   huddled in an upstairs room.
   He whose word inspired creation
   can't be silenced by the tomb

3. Christ has risen to companion
   former friends who feared the night,
   sensing loss and limitation
   where their faith had once burned bright.
   They bemoan what is no longer,
   they suspect no hopeful sign
   till Christ ends their conversation,
   breaking bread and sharing wine.

4. Christ has risen, and forever
   lives to challenge and to change
   all whose lives are messed or mangled,
   all who find religion strange.
   Christ is risen, Christ is present
   making us what he has been –
   evidence of transformation
   through which God is known and seen.

JLB & GM

Church / Holy Spirit / Worship
St Columba 8686 (CM)

COME, HOST OF HEAVEN

1. Come, Host of heaven's high dwelling place,
   come, be our honoured guest,
   and make this place your welcome home
   where lives are changed and blessed.

2. Surround these walls with faith and love
   that, through the nights and days,
   when human voices cease to speak
   the stones may echo praise.

3. Inspire in us, for Jesus' sake,
   true kindness and real peace,
   and all the joys that know the depth
   in which all sorrows cease.

4. Here may the loser find his worth,
   the stranger find a friend;
   here may the hopeless find her faith
   and aimless find their end.

5. Build, from the human fabric, signs
   of how God's kingdom thrives,
   and how the Holy Spirit changes life
   by changing lives.

6. So, to the One who holds the world
   in safe and gracious hands,
   be glory, honour, love and praise
   for which this company stands.

JLB & GM

13

Baptism
O Waly, Waly   8888 (LM)

CONCEIVER OF BOTH HEAVEN AND EARTH

1. Conceiver of both heaven and earth,
   our words are feeble to express
   the wonder of the world you bore,
   creating out of randomness.

2. Both rich and barren, damp and dry,
   you nurtured and endowed the land,
   providing with a mother's care,
   protecting with a father's hand.

3. And in your image we are made,
   and with imagination blessed;
   some may bear children, all bear fruit
   and in our love find yours expressed.

4. Be present in the gentle joy
   surrounding *this small child we* bring; *
   baptise and name *her/him* as your own
   as friends on earth and angels sing.

5. Let Christ's own love embrace *her/his* home
   and may *s/he* find *her/his* proper place –
   welcomed and wanted, listened to,
   a child of God, a gift of grace.

   Where more than one child is being baptised, this line should read 'surrounding those whom we now bring'. Thereafter, 'her/him' should then become 'them'; 'her/his' becomes 'their'; and 's/he' becomes 'they'.

JLB & GM

14 *Civic Life & Social Justice / Dismay & Distress*
Coleshill / St Anne   8686 (CM)

DO NOT BE VEXED

1. Do not be vexed or envy those
   obsessed with doing wrong.
   Their fortune is like fields of grass
   whose growth cannot last long.

2. Trust in the Lord, do what is right,
   take root in God's good ground.
   Delight in God in whose great will
   your heart's desire is found.

3. Give God your trust, and let the Lord
   direct your future way.
   The justice of your cause shall rise
   and shine as clear as day.

4. Do not be jealous or dismayed
   should evil folk succeed.
   Wait patiently for God who comes
   in quietness to your need.

5. Better the pennies of the poor
   than wicked people's gain.
   God breaks their power; but humble folk
   will never live in vain.

Paraphrase of Psalm 37: 1-7 & 16-17

JLB

Saints of God
O Waly, Waly / Tallis Canon 8888 (LM)

FOR ALL THE SAINTS

1. For all the saints who showed your love
   in how they lived and where they moved,
   for mindful women, caring men,
   accept our gratitude again.

2. For all the saints who loved your name,
   whose faith increased their Saviour's fame,
   who sang your songs and shared your word,
   accept our gratitude, good Lord.

3. For all the saints who named your will,
   and saw your kingdom coming still
   through selfless protest, prayer and praise,
   accept the gratitude we raise.

4. Bless all whose will or name or love
   reflects the grace of heaven above.
   Though unacclaimed by earthly powers,
   your life through theirs has hallowed ours.

JLB & GM

16

Marriage
Beach Spring 8787 D

FOR EACH TIME THERE IS A SEASON

1. For each time there is a season,
   for each season there's a need;
   for each passion there's a purpose,
   for each purpose there's a seed.
   Be it living, be it dying,
   moving on or standing still,
   all of life is held in tension
   and embraced by God's good will.

2. There's a time to get together
   and a time to stay alone;
   there's a time to share a future
   and yet keep what is our own.
   Every person has potential,
   every marriage is unique;
   every couple finds, in loving,
   more than they could wish or seek.

3. There's a time to wait and wonder,
   there's a time to hope and pray;
   there's a time to let commitment
   lead towards a wedding day.
   There's a time for friends to gather,
   and with them to celebrate
   love's delight and fascination
   which is God's to recreate.

4. Praise the Maker for this marriage,
   praise the Lord we can be here,
   praise the Spirit for this union –
   open, vibrant and sincere.
   Let there now be eating, dancing,
   music in the listening place,
   kindness, laughter, gentle teasing,
   firm resolve and fond embrace.

JLB

17   Holy Scripture / Human Life / Jesus Life & Ministry
Ellacombe   8686 D (DCM)

FROM ADAM CAME THE APPLE

1. From Adam came the apple,
   from Abraham the seed,
   from Noah came the floating zoo,
   from Cain the jealous deed.

   Chorus:
   > AND GOD TIED UP THE PARCEL
   > WHICH WE CALL HUMAN LIFE –
   > A BUNDLE OF ADVENTURE
   > AND LOVE AND PAIN AND STRIFE.

2. In Eve was harmless pleasure
   until she was beguiled;
   in Sarah there was envy
   until she bore a child.

   > AND GOD…

3. Take Samson and Delilah,
   take David and his wives,
   take Jesus through his ancestry –
   all show imperfect lives.

   > AND GOD…

4. In Christian and in Muslim,
   in Buddhist and Hindu,
   there lie the common fault lines
   found also in the Jew.

   > YET JESUS, WHO WAS JEWISH,
   > LOVES THOSE OF EVERY RACE,
   > FOR HE DETECTS GOD'S IMAGE
   > IN EVERY HUMAN FACE.

   (over)

JLB

5. It is not endless conflict
   but God who is our goal,
   who planned our many differences
   and yearns that we be whole.

   > O SPIRIT OF OUR MAKER
   > IN WHOM OUR HOPE IS FOUND,
   > ENABLE US TO RECOGNISE
   > THE PATHS TO COMMON GROUND.

FROM HEAVEN'S ATTENDANT HOST YOU CAME

1. From heaven's attendant host you came
   to meet and mend us on your knees;
   the saviour-servant, still you plead,
   'To know me, love the least of these.'

2. And then to show the way, you turn
   to those who do not know you yet,
   and those whose value none have seen
   or many see but soon forget.

3. Within the Church, built on your word,
   the call to care finds central place.
   Thus humble faith and human skill
   combine, through you, as means of grace.

4. To this vocation now enlist
   those in whose lives Christ is confessed;
   inform each mind, inspire each heart,
   through them may heaven and earth be blessed.

5. On every shoulder lay your hands
   confirm the calling none deserves,
   till all we say and all we do
   reflect the saviour whom we serve.

JLB & GM

19   *Advent / Christmas*
                    Wer Nur Den Lieben Gott (Neumark)   98 98 88

GIVE US, THIS YEAR

1. Give us, this year, an adult Christmas
   since among adults first you came:
   not in a creche or kindergarden
   you showed your face and learned your name.
   Then let our adult lives attest
   that childlike trust you reckon best.

2. Give us, this year, a worldly Christmas
   since it was to this world you came,
   sent to redeem all earthly matter,
   while fastened in a human frame.
   Then, for creation, help us share
   your kindly gaze, your constant care.

3. Give us, this year, a peaceful Christmas
   since as the Prince of Peace you came.
   Still jealous Herods call for slaughter,
   still Caesars play their power game.
   When will earth's politics portray
   peace is no prize? Peace is the way!

4. And give us time for you, this Christmas,
   since into time for us you came,
   bringing the voice that forged creation
   where it might gently say our name.
   Then let our hearts rejoice and sing,
   'Glory to God for everything.'

JLB

GO, SILENT FRIEND

1. Go, silent friend, your life has found its ending;
   to dust returns your weary, mortal frame.
   God, who before birth called you into being,
   now calls you hence, his accent still the same.
   Go, silent friend, your life in Christ is buried;
   for you he lived and died and rose again.
   Close by his side your promised place is waiting,
   where, fully known, you shall with God remain.

2. Go, silent friend. Forgive us if we grieved you;
   safe now in heaven, kindly say our name.
   Your life has touched us, that is why we mourn you;
   our lives without you cannot be the same.
   Go, silent friend. We do not grudge you glory.
   Sing, sing with joy deep praises to your Lord.
   You, who believed that Christ would come back for you,
   now celebrate that Jesus keeps his word.

JLB & GM

21 — Baptism
Chartres / Hyfrydol 8787 D

GOD AND PARENT OF ALL PEOPLE

1. God and parent of all people,
   maker of both heaven and earth,
   praise and gratitude we offer
   for the world you brought to birth.
   Nature in its finest clothing,
   science in its richest find
   witness your surpassing goodness,
   meant to nourish humankind.

2. Jesus Christ, eternal Saviour,
   once a child on Mary's breast,
   born to save the saint and sinner,
   destined to reveal God's best,
   you found praise in children's voices,
   you blessed babies by your touch;
   you declare for every infant
   how God loves each one so much.

3. Holy Spirit, sent among us,
   binding earth to heaven above,
   you inspire that selfless beauty
   seen where people share their love.
   For the fruits of human passion
   in the womb, the world, the heart,
   we express, as Christ's own family,
   gratitude in every part.

4. God, be present in our worship,
   welcoming the one(s) we bring;
   as we baptise, through your Spirit
   seal the grace of which we sing.
   Let our prayers and heaven's intention
   hallow water, sign and vow;
   bless *this child** whose life is offered
   to embody your life now.

* Substitute 'each child' when more than one are being baptised.

JLB

GOD BEYOND GLORY

1. God beyond glory,
   gracious and holy,
   in whose own image each life is made,
   love is the treasure,
   love is the measure
   of all your Son on earth displayed.

2. Binding each other –
   father to mother,
   parents to children, and friend to friend –
   love in its sharing,
   love in its caring,
   shows true affection none dare end.

3. Here in your presence,
   love is the essence
   sealing the vows shared by husband and wife.
   This love confessing,
   grant them your blessing
   to guard and guide their future life.

4. When joys are deepest,
   where paths are steepest,
   whatever figures in years to come,
   let loving duty
   and love in beauty
   embrace their hearts, their hopes, their home.

JLB & GM

23 *Death & Bereavement / Illness & Healing*
Gerontius / Land Of Rest 8686 (CM)

GOD, GIVE US LIFE

1. God, give us life should death seem close
   to friends we fear to lose,
   and nothing said can calm the dread
   of sad, unwanted news.

2. God, give us love in heart and hand
   to hold the hurting one,
   to free the anger, meet the need
   and wait till waiting's done.

3. God, give us skill, insight and will
   to find, where none are sure,
   new ways to mend the web of life,
   new means to heal and cure.

4. God, give us faith when loving touch
   gives way to letting go.
   Help us believe that those who leave
   still live and love and grow.

5. Then, in the end, make death a friend,
   and give us strength to stand
   and walk to where no eye can stare,
   but Christ can clasp our hand.

JLB & GM

Commitment / Holy Scripture / Saints of God
Holy Manna / Lewis Air   8787 D

GOD IT WAS

1. God it was who said to Abram,
   'Pack your bags and travel on.'
   God it was who said to Sarah,
   'Smile, and soon you'll bear a son.'
   Travelling folk and aged mothers,
   wandering when they thought they'd done –
   this is how we find God's people,
   leaving all because of One.

2. God it was who said to Moses,
   'Save my people, part the sea!'
   God it was who said to Miriam,
   'Sing and dance to show you're free.'
   Shepherd-saints and tambourinists,
   doing what God knew they could –
   this is how we find God's people,
   liberating what they should.

3. God it was who said to Joseph,
   'Down your tools and take your wife.'
   God it was who said to Mary,
   'In your womb I'll start my life.'
   Carpenter and country maiden,
   leaving town and trade and skills –
   this is how we find God's people,
   moved by what their Maker wills.

4. Christ it was who said, 'Zaccheus,
   I would like to dine with you.'
   Christ it was who said to Martha,
   'Listening's what you need to do.'
   Civil servants and housekeepers,
   changing places at a cost –
   this is how Christ summons people
   calling both the loved and lost.

(over)

JLB & GM

5. In this crowd which spans the ages
   with these saints whom we revere,
   God wants us to share their purpose
   starting now and starting here.
   So we celebrate our calling,
   so we raise both heart and voice
   as we pray that through our living
   more may find they are God's choice.

GOD LOVED THE WORLD SO MUCH

1. God loved the world so much –
   this we know, this we know;
   God loved the world so much – this we know;
   God loved the world so much,
   the world not just the church,
   that Christ came into touch, into time, into view
   declaring he would make all things new.

2. When people heard his voice,
   all were changed, all were changed;
   when people heard his voice all were changed;
   when people heard his voice,
   some rankled, some rejoiced:
   he came to vindicate what was right, to clear sight,
   expose deceit and spread truth and light.

3. The wretched of the earth
   he embraced, he embraced,
   the wretched of the earth he embraced;
   the sick and sad and poor
   he led to heaven's door.
   And there, beside the fearful and flawed, overawed,
   they felt the warmth and welcome of God.

4. On earth itself he sowed
   seeds of peace, seeds of peace;
   on earth itself he sowed seeds of peace;
   and for the world, its health,
   its wisdom and its wealth,
   he broke the bread of heaven and he shared it around
   that justice might pervade common ground.

   (over)

5. Shall we who bear his name,
   stay the same, stay the same?
   Shall we who bear his name stay the same?
   Or shall we turn our face
   towards a different place
   and, hearing words of grace meant for all, great and small,
   respond to Jesus' promise and call?

6. To God we give ourselves,
   body, mind, heart and soul;
   to God we give our mind, heart and soul.
   O Jesus, now instil
   a passion for your will
   to love all people and, in our care of the earth,
   walk in your way and cherish our worth.

Commitment / Confirmation / Holy Trinity / Worship
Bunessan   5554 D

GOD OUR CREATOR

1. God our Creator,
   you in love made us
   who once were nothing
   but now have grown.
   We bring the best
   of all our lives offer;
   for you we share
   whatever we own.

2. O Christ our Saviour,
   you in love called us
   who once were no-one,
   and felt unknown.
   We pledge to go
   wherever you summon,
   making your will and
   purpose our own.

3. O God the Spirit,
   you in love move us
   who once were nowhere,
   far from our home.
   We know our need of
   you for companion;
   all things can change
   when not on our own.

4. And with the people
   summoned together
   to be the Church in which
   faith is sown,
   we make our promise
   to live for Jesus,
   and let the world know
   all are God's own.

JLB & GM

Creation / Human Life
Thornbury 7676

27

GOD'S IS A WORLD OF BEAUTY

1. God's is a world of beauty
   in land and sea and air;
   aesthetics born in heaven
   the ocean depths declare.
   Both harmony and discord
   emerge from mother earth,
   while sunset sky and thunder
   proclaim their Maker's worth.

2. God's is a world of beauty
   in creatures and in kind;
   diversity and contrast
   reveal God's lively mind.
   In intellect and language,
   in gender and in race,
   our differences bear witness
   to variegated grace.

3. As God is our Creator
   and all God's image bear,
   we each are blessed with talents
   to treasure and to share.
   Thus painter, potter, poet,
   composer, sculptor, mime
   enable form and beauty
   in symbol, sound and time.

4. We thank you, Holy Spirit,
   for all that you inspire,
   for unattained perfection
   to which we still aspire;
   and for Jesus our Saviour,
   whose crafted words reveal
   divine imagination,
   and truth forever real.

JLB

28 *Christian Unity / Church / Holy Spirit / Pentecost*
Sussex Carol 88 88 88

GOD'S SPIRIT CAME AT PENTECOST

1. God's Spirit came at Pentecost
   to folk who feared their hope was lost;
   inspired by wind and fire of grace,
   they faced a crowded market place.
   There, speaking tongues unlike their own,
   they preached the Gospel Christ made known.

2. A multiracial audience heard
   what God through the apostles said.
   Some scorned the depths to which they'd sunk
   while others laughed and called them drunk.
   Yet many who had come to mock
   found faith in Christ, the solid rock.

3. Even now, as on that earliest day,
   we feel uncertain. So we pray:
   Lord, give us Pentecost again
   through city square and country glen.
   With or without new tongues of flame
   make your church worthy of your name.

4. Now blest be God who, through his son,
   calls unlike people to be one;
   and blest be Christ, ascended Lord,
   by heaven's community adored.
   And bless the Spirit who, on earth,
   brings all God's promises to birth.

JLB & GM

29   *Discipleship / Holy Spirit / Pentecost*
Hanover / Laudate Dominum   10 10 11 11

GOD'S SPIRIT IS HERE

1. God's Spirit is here
   that never alone
   the followers of Christ
   need face the unknown.
   The fount of all living
   is leading the dance,
   dismantling old systems
   that earth might advance.

2. She banishes sin,
   eradicates fear,
   lets hesitant faith
   affirm God is here
   till, living like Jesus
   and blessed by his name,
   we bind up the broken
   and lift up the lame.

3. She defuses hate
   and raises the dead,
   becalming life's storms,
   removing all dread.
   So that we might serve God
   confirmed from above,
   she tests us with fire
   and aflames us with love.

4. So, seek out the lost
   and share out the pain,
   and love at such cost
   that all rise again.
   God's lamplighting spirit
   is dancing the way
   from dark into dawning,
   from night into day.

JLB

30   Human Life / Life After Death / Penitence
Love Unknown   66 66 88

HELP US ACCEPT THE PAST

1. Help us accept the past:
   its pleasure, pride and pain,
   the promises fulfilled
   and vows we made in vain,
   the hidden depths we rarely knew,
   the brokenness through which we grew.

2. Help us redeem the past,
   and help us to forgive
   ourselves and all the hurt
   we're tempted to relive,
   the ones who nursed adversity
   or scorned our fallibility.

3. Help us to leave the past
   yet not to close the door,
   to live with our regrets
   but seek revenge no more.
   Let memories be trouble-free
   and dreams discover liberty.

4. Lord, thank you for the past,
   and keep it in your care
   until, released from earth,
   we enter heaven where
   the dimly seen is clearly shown,
   and we shall know as we are known.

JLB

HOW CAN WE STAND TOGETHER?

1. How can we stand together
   if we don't agree to meet?
   Why should we walk in circles
   if no fetters bind our feet?
   How dare we talk of losing
   when defeat is far from sure?
   How can the Lord be neutral
   when the privileged fleece the poor?

2. 'Stand up,' says God, 'and see the crime
   which subtly stalks the land.
   Integrity is not a word
   the powerful understand.
   The mansions of the rich are blessed
   by state and sinecure.
   And shall the Lord be neutral
   when the privileged fleece the poor?'

3. 'The sound of empty praise and prayer
   which drowns the cries of need;
   the masquerade of charity
   which covers up for greed;
   the lust to do what's "proper" –
   these are things I won't endure.
   Shall I, the Lord, be neutral
   when the privileged fleece the poor?'

4. Because he came among us,
   washed our feet and broke our bread;
   because he sat with beggars
   and ensured that all were fed;
   because he dared to question laws
   which caused more hurt than cure,
   we see God can't be neutral
   when the privileged fleece the poor.

JLB & GM

5. So, let us stand together
   as in Jesus' name we meet;
   no longer treading circles,
   we'll walk close behind his feet.
   Nor shall we talk of losing
   since the faithfulness is sure
   of Christ, the King of Heaven
   and the Saviour of the Poor.

   Paraphrase of words in the minor prophets Amos and Micah

32   Commitment / Confirmation / Holy Communion / Penitence
An Coineachan (Highland Fairy Lullaby) 8887 & Chorus

I COME IN FAITH AND FEAR TO GOD

1. I come in faith and fear to God,
   to share his feast, to hear his word,
   and meet my saviour, friend and Lord
   who bids me call him Jesus.

   Chorus:
      ALLELUIA, ALLELUIA,
      ALLELUIA, GLORY BE TO JESUS.

2. I come with shame for what I've been,
   for what I've left undone, unseen,
   for what I never meant to mean,
   for what discredits Jesus.

3. I come because God knows my name
   and welcomes me, despite my shame,
   forgiving all so I might claim
   companionship with Jesus.

4. I come because God asks me to,
   proclaiming 'This is meant for you.'
   And I believe God's word is true,
   made visible in Jesus.

5. I come and take God's life in mine
   as, in the ancient sacred sign
   of broken bread and new-poured wine,
   I taste the grace of Jesus.

6. O loving God, let me receive
   your very self and so believe
   that we are one. Then give me leave
   to live again for Jesus.

JLB

33

Faith / God's Grace / Lent & Passiontide
Martyrdom (Fenwick) / Land Of Rest   8686 (CM)

I LOVE THE LORD

1. I love the Lord because he heard
   my deep and earnest prayer.
   All that I hold within my heart
   God listens to with care.

2. I felt ensnared by chains of death,
   hell had me in its grasp;
   distress, anxiety and fear
   were all my hands could clasp.

3. And then I cried out to the Lord,
   'O God, deliver me.'
   To God, the merciful I cried
   whose faithful love sets free.

4. The Lord delivered me from death
   and dried my eyes of tears;
   God kept my feet from losing grip
   and quietened all my fears.

5. What shall I offer to the Lord
   for all the good that came?
   I'll lift salvation's holy cup
   and gladly bless God's name.

This text is especially appropriate on Maundy Thursday as Psalm 116 was commonly sung at the Passover Meal.

Paraphrase of Psalm 116

JLB

Holy Trinity / Praise of God
Brother James' Air   8686 (CM)

I OWE MY LORD A MORNING SONG

1. I owe my Lord a morning song
   for God has made this day.
   Through fears of night and hidden light
   God moves and wills my way. *

2. I owe my Lord a morning song
   for Jesus rose at dawn;
   he made death die and would not lie
   that others might live on. *

3. I owe my Lord a morning song;
   the Spirit gave me voice,
   nor did she force my soul to praise
   but honoured me with choice. *

4. I owe my Lord a morning song.
   how can I help but sing
   when God is all in all, and I
   am one with everything? *

   *When sung to Brother James' Air, repeat the last two lines of each verse.

JLB

35

Civic Life & Social Justice / Jesus' Life & Ministry
Kingsfold   8686 D

THE BEGGAR

1. I sit outside the rich world's gate,
   I rake the rich world's dross,
   and marvel that my poverty
   is what you call my cross.

   Chorus:
   OH WHO HAS EARS TO HEAR MY CRY?
   AND WHO HAS EYES TO SEE?
   AND WHO WILL LIFT MY HEAVY LOAD?
   AND WHO WILL SET ME FREE?

2. My plea is for my starving child
   in want and hunger born;
   though seed is sown, the earth remains
   too barren to grow corn.

3. My work and wisdom are employed
   to harvest others' wealth.
   A stranger on my native soil,
   I lose both heart and health.

4. My image is on every face,
   my voice in every land;
   and yet I go misunderstood
   by those who 'understand'.

5. I am the beggar called your Lord,
   the squatter called your King;
   I am the Saviour of the world,
   a torn and tattered thing.

6. So, love or leave me as you wish
   but, if you seek my will,
   you'll take my hurt into your heart
   and cease from standing still.

JLB & GM

36   *Faith / God's Grace*
                                New Britain (Amazing Grace)   8686 (CM)

I WAITED PATIENTLY FOR GOD

1. I waited patiently for God
   for God to hear my prayer;
   and God bent down to where I sank
   and listened to me there.

2. God raised me from a miry pit,
   from mud and sinking sand,
   and set my feet upon a rock
   where I can firmly stand.

3. And on my lips a song was put,
   a new song to the Lord.
   Many will marvel, open-eyed,
   and put their trust in God.

4. Great wonders you have done, O Lord,
   all purposed for our good.
   Unable every one to name,
   I bow in gratitude.

                                         Paraphrase of Psalm 40

37   Civic Life & Social Justice / Discipleship / Jesus' Life & Ministry
Salley Gardens   7676 D

INSPIRED BY LOVE AND ANGER

1. Inspired by love and anger,
   disturbed by need and pain,
   informed of God's own bias,
   we ask this once again:
      'How long must some folk suffer?
      How long can few folk mind?
      How long dare vain self-interest
      turn prayer and pity blind?'

2. From those forever victims
   of heartless human greed,
   their cruel plight composes
   a litany of need:
      'Where are the fruits of justice?
      Where are the signs of peace?
      When is the day when prisoners
      and dreams find their release?'

3. God asks, 'Who will go for me?
   Who will extend my reach?
   And who, when few will listen,
   will prophesy and preach?
   And who, when few will welcome,
   will offer all they know?
   And who, when few will follow,
   will walk the road I show?'

4. Amused in someone's kitchen,
   asleep in someone's boat,
   attuned to what the ancients
   exposed, proclaimed and wrote,
   a saviour without safety,
   a tradesman without tools
   has come to tip the balance
   with fishermen and fools.

JLB & GM

38 Civic Life & Social Justice / Interfaith Issues / Jesus' Life & Ministry
Gonfalon Royal / Agincourt (Deo Gracias) 8888 (LM)

FELLOW TRAVELLERS

1. Is God, who made and loves the earth,
   who gave each self and star its birth,
   convinced that Christians know it all?
   Or is that image much too small?

2. Did Jesus Christ, the faithful Jew,
   claim God was fond of just a few,
   content to serve a chosen race
   and limit heaven's warm embrace?

3. Did Christ not show immense respect
   for those of a less favoured sect,
   enjoying, when the faith shone clear,
   the faithful other people fear?

4. Do we presume the Muslim mind,
   what Buddhists claim or Hindus find
   is purely human in design,
   detached from all that is divine?

5. God, bless the faith we call our own,
   each word we love, each seed you've sown;
   yet humble us till we believe
   you are much more than we conceive.

6. Encourage us to look with care
   on sacred gifts which others share –
   our fellow-travellers led by light,
   who walk by faith and not by sight.

JLB

39   Discipleship / Holy Communion / Worship
Lewis Air / Blaenwern   8787 D

JESUS CALLS US

1. Jesus calls us here to meet him
   as, through word and song and prayer,
   we affirm God's promised presence
   where his people live and care.
   Praise the God who keeps each promise,
   praise the Son who calls us friends,
   praise the Spirit who, among us,
   to our hopes and fears attends.

2. Jesus calls us to confess him
   Word of life and Lord of all,
   sharer of our flesh and frailness,
   saving all who fail or fall.
   Tell his holy, human story;
   tell his tales that all may hear;
   tell the world that Christ in glory
   came to earth to meet us here.

3. Jesus calls us to each other,
   vastly different though we are;
   creed and colour, class and gender
   neither limit nor debar.
   Join the hand of friend and stranger,
   join the hands of age and youth,
   join the faithful and the doubter
   in their common search for truth.

4. Jesus calls us to his table
   rooted firm in time and space,
   where the Church in earth and heaven
   finds a common meeting place.
   Share the bread and wine, his body;
   share the love of which we sing;
   share the feast for saints and sinners
   hosted by our Lord and King.

JLB & GM

40

Easter
Noel Nouvelet 11 11 10 11

JESUS CHRIST IS RISEN

1. Jesus Christ is risen, risen from the tomb,
   he whom God conceived within the virgin's womb.
   No longer dead, redundant in the grave,
   Jesus walks the world he died in love to save.

2. Jesus Christ is risen, snares of hell are burst;
   God's own son has conquered human nature's worst.
   All sinful souls can be, by Christ, forgiven;
   earth is meant to share the grace enjoyed by heaven.

3. Jesus Christ is risen, let his foes take note;
   force can no more frighten, greed can no more gloat.
   Tyrants should tremble, avarice should cower;
   naked love has triumphed over worldly power.

4. Jesus Christ is risen and will soon ascend
   where space finds its limit and time meets its end.
   Yet throughout earth his Spirit will remain
   raising life from death like growth from fallen grain.

JLB

Discipleship / Jesus' Life & Ministry
Noel Nouvelet   11 11 10 11

JESUS CHRIST IS WAITING

1. Jesus Christ is waiting,
   waiting in the streets,
   no one is his neighbour,
   all alone he eats.
   Listen, Lord Jesus,
   I am lonely too;
   make me, friend or stranger,
   fit to wait on you.

2. Jesus Christ is raging,
   raging in the streets
   where injustice spirals
   and real hope retreats.
   Listen, Lord Jesus,
   I feel anger too;
   in the Kingdom's causes
   let me rage with you.

3. Jesus Christ is healing,
   healing in the streets,
   curing those who suffer,
   touching those he greets.
   Listen, Lord Jesus,
   I have pity too;
   let my care be active,
   healing just like you.

4. Jesus Christ is dancing,
   dancing in the streets
   where each sign of hatred
   he, with love, defeats.
   Listen, Lord Jesus,
   I should triumph too;
   where good conquers evil
   let me dance with you.

(over)

JLB & GM

5. Jesus Christ is calling,
   calling in the streets,
   'Who will join my journey?
   I will guide your feet.'
   Listen, Lord Jesus,
   let my fears be few;
   walk one step before me,
   I will follow you.

Change / Easter
O Waly, Waly / Suantrai 8888 (LM)

JESUS WAS DOUBTED

1. Jesus was doubted when he said
   that he would rise up from the dead,
   until, released from mortal pain,
   he rose to live and love again.

2. God's Spirit moves across the earth
   bringing potential to its birth,
   revealing truth, disarming lies,
   enabling buried hope to rise.

3. We are not here to stay the same,
   to leave this world as when we came.
   Some things must die, some systems fail,
   the powerless thrive, the powerful quail.

4. 'All things must change and be made new' –
   if this is strange it first is true.
   God wills a new heaven to appear
   among the ashes of life here.

JLB

Dismay & Distress / Illness & Healing
Hesperus / O Waly, Waly   8888 (LM)

JUST AS A LOST AND THIRSTY DEER

1. Just as a lost and thirsty deer
   longs for a cool and running stream,
   I thirst for you, the living God,
   anxious to know that you are near.

2. Both day and night I cry aloud;
   tears have become my only food
   while all around cruel voices ask,
   'Where is your God? Where is your God?'

3. Broken and hurt I call to mind
   how in the past I served the Lord,
   worshipped and walked with happy crowds
   singing and shouting praise to God.

4. Why am I now so lost and low?
   Why am I troubled and confused?
   Given no answer, still I hope
   and trust my Saviour and my God.

Paraphrase of Psalm 42

JLB & GM

44

Faith / God's Grace / Joy
Hyfrydol   8787 D

KEEP ME, LORD

1. Keep me, Lord, for in your keeping
   I have found security;
   and, rejoicing in your presence,
   know and own my destiny.
   You, my God, my cup, my portion
   plot my lifeline, chart my days;
   well content with where you place me,
   all your providence I praise.

2. I shall bless the Lord for giving
   sound advice for broad daylight;
   wisdom for my inmost being
   God communicates by night.
   So I set the Lord before me
   holding fast to each command;
   disregarding what dares shake me,
   God I keep at my right hand.

3. Therefore body, mind and spirit
   in serenity abound;
   death and hell can never menace
   those whose faith in God is found.
   You, O gracious Lord, will show me
   paths to all you have in store;
   in your presence, in your purpose,
   pleasures last for evermore.

Paraphrase of Psalm 16

JLB

45   *Praise Of God*
Duke Street / Tallis Canon   8888 (LM)

LET EVERY NATION ON THE EARTH

1. Let every nation on the earth
   praise God whose love brought all to birth.
   Come close to God with joyful songs,
   to whom our highest praise belongs.

2. Be certain: God alone is Lord;
   life came from his creative Word.
   Our lives are meant; God's mark we bear;
   like pastured sheep we're led with care.

3. Be glad to enter heaven's gates,
   as lively worship celebrates
   the gratitude we gladly bring,
   the offering of praise we sing.

4. Know God is Lord and God is good;
   God's grace evokes our gratitude;
   God's love and loyalty extend
   to every age, world without end.

Paraphrase of Psalm 100

JLB

Discipleship / God's Grace / Love
Dominus Regit Me / St Columba 8787

LONG HAVE YOU LOVED ME

1. Long have you loved me, Holy God:
   in love my life was knitted,*
   my self was shaped, my soul was weaned,
   my fate and future fitted.*

2. Long have you loved me, Holy God,
   and freely did you fashion
   my mind, my heart, my will, my skill,
   my hesitance and passion.

3. Long have you loved me, Holy God,
   and yearned for closer bonding
   that through naught else but love, my love
   to yours might come responding.

4. Long have you loved me, Holy God;
   too long have I resisted.
   Now late I come, though from the start,
   my life in yours existed.

5. So take and make me yours, through Christ
   in whom all are perfected;
   and reap the harvest of the seed
   you sowed and resurrected.

6. Long will I love you, Holy God:
   more yet will I discover
   of who I am and who you are,
   my destiny and lover.

   When the tune 'St Columba' is used, the last note of lines 2 and 4 in each verse is repeated.

JLB

Commitment / Confirmation / Lent & Passiontide
Ye Banks and Braes 8888 D (DLM)

LORD JESUS CHRIST, SHALL I STAND STILL?

1. Lord Jesus Christ, shall I stand still
   and stare at you hung on the tree;
   or shall I follow where you call
   and show the path to life for me?
   Shall I to sin and failure cling
   consorting with the guilt I hate;
   or on your shoulders shall I fling
   the wrong I breed and contemplate?

2. Shall I your story read and tell
   to note your mark on history;
   or shall I make your story mine
   and live by faith and mystery?
   Shall I embrace the love you show
   and covet this sweet, holy thing;
   or of that love shall my heart speak,
   my hands relate, my being sing?

3. Shall I retreat from where you fall
   and seek a safer path through life;
   or shall I meet you in the world
   where peace is scarce, injustice rife?
   Lord Jesus Christ, the God who lives
   to love and die and rise again,
   make me the who, and you the why,
   your love the how, and now the when.

JLB & GM

48   Lent & Passiontide / Penitence
Eventide   10 10 10 10

LORD, WHEN YOUR KINGDOM COMES

1. Lord, when your kingdom comes, remember me
   not like the dying thief upon the tree
   but as a living struggler with your will
   who, in the midst of doubt, believed you still.

2. Lord, when your kingdom comes, remember me;
   perceive, behind the front which others see,
   each of my soul's dark nights, the trust betrayed
   and all for which I wrestled, fought and prayed.

3. Lord, when your kingdom comes, remember me
   puzzled by what I am and am to be,
   hindered by fears too great and faith too small,
   yet fascinated by you through it all.

4. Lord, when your kingdom comes, remember me –
   anger and passion, joy and jealousy.
   I would not have you love what I am not,
   since in your net all that I am is caught.

5. If, as you said, your kingdom now is here,
   though its complete design remains unclear,
   let this one life discover its true place
   as more of me is transformed by your grace.

MONARCH AND MAKER

1. Monarch and maker of all time and space,
   sculptor of mountain and of desert place,
   source and sustainer of both sea and land,
   all that exists was crafted by your hand.

2. Yours are the myriad stars and cosmic grace,
   yours is the image in each human face;
   history and mystery in all that we know,
   yours is the love through which we live and grow.

3. Help us as guardians of all life on earth
   both to respect the world and prize its worth;
   and, in deep gratitude for all you give,
   turn greed to sharing so that all may live.

4. Glory to God to whom all praise is due,
   glory to Jesus making all things new,
   glory to God the Spirit, bold and bright,
   who leads the world through darkness into light.

JLB

50

Advent
Columcille 6565 D

NO WIND AT THE WINDOW

1. No wind at the window,
   no lock on the door;
   no light from the lamp stand,
   no foot on the floor;
   no dream born of tiredness,
   no ghost raised by fear;
   just an angel and a woman
   and a voice in her ear.

2. 'Oh Mary, oh Mary,
   don't hide from my face.
   Be glad that you're favoured
   and filled with God's grace.
   The time for redeeming
   the world has begun;
   and you are requested
   to mother God's son.

3. 'This child must be born
   that the kingdom might come –
   salvation for many,
   destruction for some;
   both end and beginning,
   both message and sign,
   both victor and victim,
   both yours and divine.'

4. No payment was promised,
   no promises made;
   no wedding was dated,
   no blueprint displayed.
   Yet Mary, consenting
   to what none could guess,
   replied with conviction,
   'Tell God I say yes.'

JLB

Christmas
Gott Will's Machen 8787

THE PEDIGREE

1. Not the powerful, not the privileged,
   not the famous in the land,
   but the no-ones and the needy
   were the first to hold God's hand.

2. Not a well-established family
   with an heirloom christening shawl,
   but a homeless, wandering couple
   parented the Lord of All.

3. Not at first to little children
   nor to those whose faith burned bright,
   but to adults, stalled in darkness,
   angels brought God's love and light.

4. God, determined to be different
   from the standards we think best,
   in his choice of friends and family
   lets forgotten folk be blessed.

5. Not obsessed by our achievements,
   worldly wealth or family tree,
   may we, in and with God's chosen,
   find our fondest pedigree.

JLB

52   Faith / God's Grace / Holy Communion
Liebster Jesu 78 78 88

NOT THROUGH MERIT

1. Not through merit, not through skill,
   nor through wealth or education,
   but because God knows our need
   and extends the invitation,
   we can gather round this table,
   here for all God will enable.

2. Other feasts select their guests,
   other hosts can seem elusive;
   other gatherings remain
   self-selecting and exclusive.
   Here, to all God loves, is given
   food from earth refined by heaven.

3. Come, O Holy Spirit come!
   As we do what Christ has bidden,
   draw us closer to our Lord,
   ever here yet ever hidden.
   Let this bread and wine, in essence,
   be for us his living presence.

4. Here renew and here affirm,
   redirect us and restore us;
   here unite us with the saints,
   those we love who went before us.
   As we hold them in affection,
   steer our lives in their direction.

5. Glory be to God above,
   always holy, always other.
   Glory be to Jesus Christ,
   heavenly monarch, earthly brother.
   Glory to the Holy Spirit
   who reveals all we inherit.

JLB

Death & Bereavement / Jesus' Life & Ministry
Rockingham   8888 (LM)

O CHRIST, YOU WEPT

1. O Christ, you wept when grief was raw,
   and felt for those who mourned their friend;
   come close to where we would not be
   and hold us, numbed by this life's end.

2. The well-loved voice is silent now
   and there is much we meant to say;
   collect our lost and wandering words
   and keep them till the endless day.

3. We try to hold what is not here
   and fear for what we do not know;
   oh, take our hands in yours, good Lord,
   and free us to let our friend go.

4. In all our loneliness and doubt,
   through what we cannot realise,
   address us from your empty tomb
   and tell us that life never dies.

JLB & GM

54

Advent / God's Majesty
Forest Green   8686 D (DCM)

O GOD, WITH HOLY RIGHTEOUSNESS

1. O God, with holy righteousness
   sustain your royal son,
   that he may help your suffering folk
   and see your justice done.
   Through all the earth, from shore to shore,
   his kingdom shall extend;
   his enemies shall lick the dust,
   his reign shall never end.

2. Rulers and kings of every land
   shall bow before his throne;
   and all the nations of the world
   shall make his will their own.
   For he shall rescue those in need,
   protect the frightened poor
   and, in the face of every threat,
   make fragile lives secure.

3. Long may his name last like the sun,
   long be his fame expressed
   as people for like blessing pray
   who know him as God's blessed.
   And blessed be God, for God alone
   brings wondrous things to birth;
   for ever may God's name be praised
   whose glory fills the earth.

Paraphrase of Psalm 72

JLB

55   *Faith*
Coe Fen / Resignation   8686 D (DCM)

O GOD, YOU ARE MY GOD ALONE

1. O God, you are my God alone
   whom eagerly I seek,
   though longing fills my soul with thirst
   and leaves my body weak.
   Just like a dry and barren land
   awaits a freshening shower,
   I long within your house to see
   your glory and your power.

2. Your faithful love surpasses life,
   evoking all my praise.
   Through every day, to bless your name,
   my hands in joy I'll raise.
   My deepest need you satisfy
   as with a sumptuous feast.
   So, on my lips and in my heart,
   your praise has never ceased.

3. Throughout the night I lie in bed
   and call you, Lord, to mind;
   in darkest hours I meditate
   how God, my strength, is kind.
   Beneath the shadow of your wing,
   I live and feel secure;
   and daily, as I follow close,
   your right hand keeps me sure.

Paraphrase of Psalm 63

JLB

Creation / Praise Of God
Ellacombe 8686 D

O LORD, OUR LORD

1. O Lord, our Lord, throughout the earth
   how glorious is your name;
   and glorious too where unseen heavens
   your majesty proclaim.
   On infant lips, in children's song
   a strong defence you raise
   to counter enemy and threat
   and foil the rebel's ways.

2. When I look up and see the sky
   which your own fingers made,
   and wonder at the moon and stars
   each perfectly displayed,
   then I must ask, 'Why do you care?
   Why love humanity?
   And why keep every mortal name
   fixed in your memory?'

3. Yet such as us you made and meant
   just less than gods to be;
   with honour and with glory, Lord,
   you crowned humanity.
   And then dominion you bestowed
   for all made by your hand:
   all sheep and cattle, birds and fish
   that move through sea and land.

   Coda (for which repeat last four bars of tune):

   O Lord, our Lord, throughout the earth
   how glorious is your name!

Paraphrase of Psalm 8

JLB

57   Human Life / Love / Marriage
Love Unknown 66 66 88

THE WEB OF LOVE

1. Of all that we enjoy
   in harmony with heaven,
   of all our hearts desire,
   of all received and given,
   we cherish most the web God wove
   of costly and inclusive love.

2. Such diverse threads combine
   in woman and in man:
   Ruth pledged to Naomi,
   David to Jonathan;
   John laid his head on Jesus' breast
   whose feet a woman's tears caressed.

3. And Paul, with special care,
   chose poetry over prose
   to celebrate how love affirms,
   endures and grows,
   believes the best, embraces pain,
   survives through death to rise again.

4a. So we delight today
    to gather in this place
    as two we cherish pledge to love
    and live by grace.
    God, partner them through what's to come,
    and bless their hearts, their hopes, their home

4b. God, make all Christians bold
    to live and love by grace,
    and nurture deep affection
    in this holy place.
    Help all believers to be true
    to how you made them and to you.

Verse 4a is specifically for the blessing of a marriage or partnership. 4b is for general use.

JLB

OH WHERE ARE YOU GOING?

1. Oh where are you going
   and can I come with you,
   and what is your method
   for keeping alive?
   No pack or possessions,
   no clothing or shelter,
   no food to sustain you –
   how can you survive?

2. Oh where are you going
   and can I come with you,
   and why is your company
   never the same?
   You sit among beggars,
   you argue with bankers,
   debate with the lawyers
   and walk with the lame.

3. Oh where are you going,
   and can I come with you,
   and what can you show
   for your talents and time –
   no profit from trading,
   no thing of your making,
   no mark or memento,
   no picture or rhyme.

4. Oh where are you going
   and can I come with you,
   and what is the secret
   towards which you strive?
   What hidden inspirer,
   what unseen admirer,
   what dream is the substance
   upon which you thrive?

(over)

5. 'I'm going on a journey
   and welcome companions,
   but don't ask me how we'll
   survive, where we'll go,
   or who will be with us
   or what we'll be doing.
   Just join me in travelling
   and learn all I know.'

59 *Dismay & Distress / Penitence*
Southwell   6686 (SM)

OUT OF THE DIREST DEPTHS

1. Out of the direst depths
   I make my earnest plea.
   O graciously bow down your ear
   and listen, Lord, to me.

2. If you kept note of sins,
   before you who could stand?
   But since forgiveness is your gift,
   our reverence you command.

3. My soul longs for the Lord,
   and yearns to hear God's word.
   More keenly than some watch for dawn,
   I wait and watch for God.

4. Yes, with the Lord is grace
   and power to free and save.
   Redemption from their every sin
   God's people shall yet have.

Paraphrase of Psalm 130

Civil Life & Social Justice / Praise of God
Laus Deo / Stuttgart 8787

PRAISE THE LORD, THE GROUND OF GOODNESS

1. Praise the Lord, the ground of goodness,
   source of silence, sound and time,
   nourisher of fed and foodless,
   catalyst of sense and rhyme.

2. Praise the Lord with city voices,
   pitched in concrete, sweat and steel,
   let the thousand urban choices
   bias to what's right and real.

3. Praise the Lord as science advances,
   research deepens, knowledge grows.
   Let such progress serve, with gladness,
   every need God shall expose.

4. Praise the Lord for honest pleasure:
   fond embrace, surprising news,
   soul-filled thought, creative treasure,
   skill to counsel or amuse.

5. Praise the Lord as churches chorus –
   Quaker-quiet, Salvation-brassed,
   Catholic, Orthodox – united,
   showing oneness meant to last.

6. Praise the Lord, the world's Creator;
   praise our host and guest, the Son;
   praise the ever-roving Spirit,
   pulse of life for everyone.

JLB & GM

Human Life / Praise of God
Slane 10 10 10 10

61

WORLD WITHOUT END

1. Praise to the Lord for the joys of the earth:
   cycles of season and reason and birth,
   contrasts in landscape and outlook and need,
   challenge of famine, pollution and greed.

2. Praise to the Lord for the progress of life:
   cradle and grave, bond of husband and wife,
   pain of youth growing and wrinkling of age,
   questions in step with experience and stage.

3. Praise to the Lord for his care of our kind:
   faith for the faithless and sight for the blind,
   healing, acceptance, disturbance and change,
   all the emotions through which our lives range.

4. Praise to the Lord for the people we meet
   safe in our homes or at risk in the street;
   kiss of a lover and friendship's embrace,
   smile of a stranger and words full of grace.

5. Praise to the Lord for the carpenter's son
   dovetailing worship and work into one;
   tradesman and teacher and vagrant and friend,
   source of all life in this world without end.

JLB & GM

62

Holy Trinity / Praise of God
Lauda Anima (Praise My Soul)   87 87 87

PRAISE WITH JOY

1. Praise with joy the world's Creator,
   God of justice, love and peace,
   source and end of human knowledge,
   force of greatness without cease.
   Celebrate the Maker's glory –
   power to rescue and release.

2. Praise the Son who feeds the hungry,
   clothes the naked, finds the lost,
   heals the sick, upsets religion,
   fearless of both fate and cost.
   Celebrate Christ's constant presence –
   friend and stranger, guest and host.

3. Praise the Spirit sent among us
   liberating truth from pride,
   forging bonds where race or gender,
   age or nation dare divide.
   Celebrate the Spirit's treasure –
   foolishness none dare deride.

4. Praise the Maker, Son and Spirit,
   one God in community,
   calling Christians to embody
   oneness and diversity.
   Thus the world shall yet believe
   when shown Christ's vibrant unity.

JLB & GM

63   *Praise of God / Truth*
Blaenwern / Ode to Joy 8787 D

SHOUT FOR JOY

1. Shout for joy, you sons and daughters,
who delight to praise God's name.
Play and strum your skilful music;
with your lips new songs proclaim.
God's own word is true and tested,
nothing can its truth remove.
Source of goodness, fount of justice,
earth is salted with God's love.

2. By command God made the heavens,
shaped and filled it with a word;
seas and clouds were brought together,
stored and gathered by the Lord.
By God's will earth was created:
God decreed and there it stood.
Let the world revere its Maker,
praising God, forever good.

3. God frustrates the plans of nations,
upsets great designs and dreams;
but his purpose stands for ever,
indestructable God's schemes.
Heaven looks down on every mortal,
all that lives on earth is known;
happy therefore are the people
whom God chooses for his own.

4. Kings are not kept safe by armies,
warriors fail despite their strength;
all the speed of powerful horses
must give out and fail at length.
True salvation greets the people
who for God's intentions strive;
these, through death and through disaster,
God will love and keep alive.

Paraphrase of Psalm 33: 1-19

JLB

64 Death & Bereavement / Dismay & Distress / Illness & Healing
Gott Will's Machen 8787

SING, MY SOUL

1. Sing, my soul, when hope is sleeping,
   sing when faith gives way to fears;
   sing to melt the ice of sadness,
   making way for joy through tears.

2. Sing, my soul, when sickness lingers,
   sing to dull the sharpest pain;
   sing to set the spirit leaping:
   healing needs a glad refrain.

3. Sing, my soul, of him who shaped me,
   let me wander far away,
   ran with open arms to greet me,
   brought me home again to stay.

4. Sing, my soul, when light seems darkest,
   sing when night refuses rest,
   sing though death should mock the future:
   what's to come by God is blessed.

JLB & GM

Creation / Praise Of God
The Vicar of Bray / How Can I Keep From Singing?   8787 D

SING PRAISE TO GOD

1. Sing praise to God on mountain tops
   and in earth's lowest places,
   from blue lagoon to polar waste,
   from ocean to oasis.
   No random rock produced this world
   but God's own will and wonder.
   Thus hills rejoice and valleys sing
   and clouds concur with thunder.

2. Sing praise to God where grasses grow
   and flowers display their beauty,
   where Nature weaves her myriad web
   through love as much as duty.
   The seasons in their cycle speak
   of earth's complete provision.
   Let nothing mock inherent good
   or treat it with derision.

3, Sing praise to God where fishes swim
   and birds fly in formation,
   where animals of every kind
   diversify creation.
   All life that finds its home on earth
   is meant to be respected.
   Let nothing threaten, for base ends,
   what God through grace perfected.

4. Sing praise to God where humankind
   its majesty embraces,
   where different races, creeds and tongues
   distinguish different faces.
   God's image in each child of earth
   shall never pale or perish.
   So treat with love each human soul
   and thus God's goodness cherish.

JLB & GM

66 *Christian Unity / Creation / Interfaith Issues*
All For Jesus / Stuttgart 8787

SING TO GOD WITH JOY AND GLADNESS

1. Sing to God with joy and gladness
   hymns and psalms of gratitude;
   with the voice of praise discover
   that to worship God is good.

2. God unites the scattered people,
   gathers those who wandered far,
   heals the hurt and broken spirits,
   tending every wound and scar.

3. Such is God's great power and wisdom
   none can calculate or tell;
   God is keen to ground the wicked
   and with humble folk to dwell.

4. God, with clouds, the sky has curtained
   thus ensuring rain will fall;
   earth, responding, grows to order
   food for creatures great and small.

5. God's discernment never favours
   strength or speed to lift or move;
   God invites us to show reverence,
   trusting in his steadfast love.

Paraphrase of Psalm 147: 1-11

67   Commitment / Confirmation / Discipleship
Gelobt Sei Gott (Vulpius)   888 12

SISTERS AND BROTHERS, WITH ONE VOICE

1. Sisters and brothers, with one voice
   confirm your calling and rejoice:
   each is God's child and each God's choice.

   Refrain:
       ALLELUIA! ALLELUIA! ALLELUIA!

2. Strangers no more, but cherished friends,
   live as the body God intends,
   sharing the love the Spirit sends.

3. Not, though, by wisdom, wealth or skill,
   nor by ourselves can we fulfil
   what, for the world, is God's own will.

4. Christ is the Way. By him alone
   seeds of the kingdom's life are sown,
   patterns of heaven on earth are shown.

5. Then follow Christ through every day;
   fear not what crowd or critics say.
   Those on the move move those who stay.

6. In factory, office, home or hall,
   where people struggle, strive or stall,
   seek out and serve the Lord of All.

7. Seeking and serving, with one voice
   confirm your calling and rejoice:
   each is God's child and each God's choice.

JLB & GM

68   Advent / Civic Life & Social Justice
Loch Lomond   11 9 11 9 D

THE DAY SOON WILL COME

1. 'The day soon will come when I'll stand by your side,
   and I'll show you my face and my favour;
   your cries I will answer, your tears I'll wipe away;
   I will guard and protect you forever.'

   Chorus:
   > LET MUSIC FILL HEAVEN
   > AND GLADNESS FILL EARTH;
   > LET THE TALL MOUNTAINS SING
   >   WITH DEEP FERVOUR,
   > FOR GOD WILL RESPOND
   > TO THE CRY OF THE POOR
   > AND WILL BANISH OPPRESSION FOREVER.

2. 'To you and to yours and to those far away
   this promise I'll make for my people:
   the fields which were barren shall flourish once again,
   and the land once abandoned I'll settle.'

3. 'Those hidden in darkness I'll call into light,
   and prisoners I'll lead into freedom;
   and none shall fear hunger and none shall suffer thirst;
   for their God, who is loving, will lead them.'

4. 'A highway across the tall mountains I'll make,
   a road I'll prepare for my people;
   from east and from west, from all corners of the earth
   I will gather the lost and the broken.'

Text based on Isaiah 49: 8-13

JLB

Change / New Year
Winchester New 8888 (LM)

THE GOD OF ALL ETERNITY

1. The God of all eternity,
   unbound by space yet always near,
   is present where his people meet
   to celebrate the coming year.

2. What shall we offer God today –
   our dreams of things that might yet be,
   or, with eyes fastened to the past,
   our dread of what we cannot see?

3. God does not share our doubts and fears,
   nor shrinks from the unknown or strange:
   the one who fashioned heaven and earth
   makes all things new and ushers change.

4. Let faith or fortune rise and fall,
   let apprehension have its day;
   those whom God loves walk unafraid
   with Christ for guide and Christ their way.

5. God grant that we, *in this new year,**
   may know and show the Kingdom's face;
   and let our work and worship thrive
   as signs of hope and means of grace.

   **When used at times other than New Year: 'throughout the year'*

JLB & GM

Advent / Christmas
Eisenach / Verbum Supernum 8888 (LM)

THE HOPE THAT HIDES IN BETHLEHEM

1. The hope that hides in Bethlehem –
   a promise hidden in the past,
   a seed an ancient sower cast –
   is meant for every us and them.

2. No silent night at Bethlehem
   as reunited friends crowd out
   the pain of birth, the mother's shout
   which heralds heaven's priceless gem.

3. No safe repose at Bethlehem:
   in earthly danger he is laid
   at whose command the world was made,
   he who is root and flower and stem.

4. The house of bread is Bethlehem,
   the birthing place of heavenly food,
   of Jesus born in flesh and blood
   with angels claiming God is good.

JLB

Church / Worship
Tallis Canon 8888 (LM)

71

THE HOUSE OF GOD

1. The House of God is our delight:
   its faith is strong, its future bright
   where doors and hearts are open wide
   and those within serve those outside.

2. The House of God is built on rock:
   Jesus and Peter, Abraham's stock
   and saints and angels who surround
   all for whom Christ is solid ground.

3. The House of God is built on prayer
   which blesses all who gather there;
   prayer which is more than quick request
   and honours Christ as gift and guest.

4. The House of God is built on love;
   such love as wills that all should move
   from past to future, guilt to grace,
   from old to new, far-off to base.

5. The House of God is built on joy,
   no sentimental cheap alloy,
   but deep delight and fervent praise
   from diverse lives in different ways.

6. God bless each House which bears your name;
   let none who enter leave the same.
   For, touched by you, all is transformed;
   and we, to Christ, are more conformed.

JLB

72   Holy Communion / Joy / Love
Love Unknown   66 66 88

THE LOVE OF GOD COMES CLOSE

1. The love of God comes close
   where stands an open door
   to let the stranger in,
   to mingle rich and poor:
   the love of God is here to stay
   embracing those who walk his way.

2. The peace of God comes close
   to those caught in the storm,
   forgoing lives of ease
   to ease the lives forlorn:
   the peace of God is here to stay
   embracing those who walk his way.

3. The joy of God comes close
   where faith encounters fears,
   where heights and depths of life
   are found through smiles and tears:
   the joy of God is here to stay
   embracing those who walk his way.

4. The grace of God comes close
   to those whose grace is spent
   where hearts are tired or sore
   and hope is bruised or bent:
   the grace of God is here to stay
   embracing those who walk his way.

5. The Son of God comes close
   where people praise his name,
   where bread and wine are blessed
   and shared as when he came; *
   the Son of God is here to stay
   embracing those who walk his way.

   * For non-Eucharistic occasions:
   where what he said is done
   with love, as when he came;

JLB & GM

73 — Faith / God's Grace
Martyrdom (Fenwick) / New Britain (Amazing Grace)   8686 (CM)

THE 'OTHER PERSON'

1. The 'other person' Jesus saw
   was one the rest despised,
   his virtues unidentified,
   her worth unrealised.

2. The 'other person' Jesus saw
   was known for what was wrong,
   not for the wrong once done to him,
   nor for her soul or song.

3. The 'other person' Jesus saw
   had faith nobody knew,
   and grounded hope and grateful love
   found only in a few.

4. The 'other person' Jesus saw
   was meant to laugh and shout,
   defy authoritarian rules
   and drive the demons out.

5. The 'other person' Jesus sees
   is also known to me:
   it's who I am beneath the masks
   and who I'm meant to be.

6. Come gently, Jesus, to our aid;
   let there be recognised
   the good each 'other' has to share,
   even when it's well disguised.

JLB

74   Abuse / Christmas / Holy Scripture
Noel 8686 D (DCM)

THE INNOCENTS

1. The soldiers fear the captain's wrath,
   the captain fears the king;
   the king is scared of who-knows-what,
   some new religious thing.
   So he commands and they obey
   and no one dares complain
   that murder, rape and cruelty
   are features of his reign.

2. The children are too young to feel
   the fear that adults show,
   the horror gnawing at their nerves
   which only mothers know.
   They hear the hurried, tramping feet,
   the snort of bated breath
   from those who beat their consciences,
   then beat a child to death.

3. He is not there – the one they want.
   His father, in a dream,
   was warned that Herod's jealousy
   would hatch a bloody scheme.
   But he who missed the massacre,
   when recognised as Lord
   will lacerate both sin and death
   with truth, his only sword.

4. It happened then in Bethlehem;
   it happens still today
   where power demands a sacrifice
   to let the powerful stay.
   And always mothers cry to God,
   for when their children die
   through war, abuse or poverty
   they rage, demanding why?

JLB

5. O hear them, God, and let them know
   that not by your design
   do tyrants prey on innocents
   while consciences resign.
   And turn our minds and hearts and hands
   until, through faith and skill,
   we leave behind our 'innocence'
   and do your holy will.

   This text is most appropriate on 28th December, the Feast of the Holy Innocents

75 Advent / Peace
Sussex Carol 88 88 88

THE TIME HAS COME

1. The time has come when, from the past,
   prophetic words ring true at last;
   though earth's hostilities increase,
   God's promise is of lasting peace.
   > Hallelujah! Prepare the way.
   > Hear what God's chosen prophets say.

2. The time has come to make it known
   that every tear and pain and groan
   are registered in heaven above
   to be redeemed by holy love.
   > Hallelujah! Prepare the way.
   > Only Love lifts us from dismay.

3. The time has come to make amends:
   earth and its people should be friends.
   Erase the policies of death,
   spread hope with every vital breath.
   > Hallelujah! Prepare the way.
   > God gladly comes to earth to stay.

4. The time has come to share good news,
   to sweep the floor and mend the shoes,
   prepare to protest, praise and dance
   for God is eager to advance.
   > Hallelujah! Expect a birth:
   > God's gracious feet will touch the earth.

JLB

Creation / Death & Bereavement
Southwell 6686 (SM)

THE WHOLE CREATION WAITS

1. The whole creation waits,
   its destiny concealed,
   till lost humanity is found
   and God's design revealed.

2. The whole creation groans
   beneath the weight of sin;
   though shackled, it anticipates
   its freedom will begin.

3. The whole creation strains:
   the universe perspires
   and struggles with the pain of birth
   as God's design requires.

4. The whole creation hopes;
   with it we yearn to be
   delivered from the labour room
   we call mortality.

5. This hope is not the wish
   to be what we have been,
   but to embrace what is not known
   and what is yet unseen.

Paraphrase of Romans 8: 19-25

Holy Scripture
Land Of Rest / St Columba 8686 (CM)

THE WORD OF GOD IS LIKE A LAMP

1. The word of God is like a lamp
   which scatters light around,
   revealing truth, rekindling youth,
   defining holy ground.

2. The word of God is like a sword
   which pierces to the core,
   disabling lies, dispelling sighs,
   to bless and never bore.

3. The word of God is like a chest
   which brims with precious gold,
   enriching all who heed God's call
   with wisdom, new and old.

4. So let us praise our gracious God
   who gave the world this word;
   and let our minds be sealed and signed
   by Jesus Christ, our Lord.

JLB

Holy Scripture / Saints of God / Women
The Seven Joys of Mary 8686 D (DCM)

THERE IS A LINE OF WOMEN

1. There is a line of women
   extending back to Eve
   whose role in shaping history
   God only could conceive;
   and though through endless ages
   their witness was repressed,
   God valued and encouraged them
   through whom the world was blessed.
   > So sing a song of Sarah –
   > to laughter she gave birth;
   > and sing a song of Tamar
   > who stood for women's worth;
   > and sing a song of Hannah
   > who bargained with her Lord;
   > and sing a song of Mary
   > who bore and bred God's Word.

2. There is a line of women
   who took on powerful men,
   defying laws and scruples
   to let life live again;
   and though, despite their triumph,
   their stories stayed untold,
   God kept their number growing,
   creative, strong and bold.
   > So sing a song of Shiphrah
   > with Puah close at hand:
   > engaged to kill male children,
   > they foiled the king's command;
   > and sing a song of Rahab
   > who sheltered spies and lied;
   > and sing a song of Esther
   > preventing genocide.

(over)

JLB

3. There is a line of women
   who stood by Jesus' side,
   who housed him while he ministered
   and held him when he died;
   and though they claimed he'd risen,
   their news was deemed suspect
   till Jesus stood among them,
   his womanly elect.
   > So sing a song of Anna
   > who saw Christ's infant face;
   > and sing a song of Martha
   > who gave him food and space;
   > and sing of all the Marys
   > who heeded his requests,
   > and now, at heaven's banquet,
   > are Jesus' fondest guests.

79

Advent
Forest Green 8686 D (DCM)

THE FIRST MIRACLE

1. There travelled Joseph and his bride
   towards the numbering,
   and on each bough the turtle doves
   and birds were chorusing.
   The two walked slowly through the groves
   till, deep inside a wood,
   they saw a tree which bore a fruit
   rasp red and very good.

2. Then spoke fair Mary to her love
   in words both low and sweet,
   'Fetch me the fruit that I desire
   that I may taste and eat.'
   But Joseph faltered to respond,
   confused and in despair,
   'Before I stretch to pull the fruit,
   tell me whose fruit you bear?'

3. Then from the womb in which he dwelt
   the babe gave this command:
   'Bow down you fair and generous boughs
   to reach my mother's hand.'
   And from the tallest to the least
   they bent to Mary's knee,
   so she could taste her favourite fruit
   from the obedient tree.

4. Then Joseph spoke as Mary ate
   to show that now he knew
   that what an angel once foretold
   had actually come true.
   'It's Him you carry in your womb –
   the glorious Lord of grace.
   Among all women, blessed are you
   who brings God face to face.'

Based on an ancient Celtic poem

JLB

Church / Worship
Was Lebet, Was Schwebet 11 10 11 10

THIS IS GOD'S HOUSE

1. This is God's house, holy ground for God's people,
   hallowed by singing and silence and prayer;
   blessed by the presence and power of the Spirit,
   founded on faith in the Saviour we share.

2. This is the place where the Church, as Christ's body,
   meets as a family where all have their place:
   stalwart and stranger, speaker and seeker –
   each needs the other and all need God's grace.

3. This is the time when desires and intentions
   find interaction with God's holy word:
   trouble and treasure and business and pleasure,
   all are redeemed and restored by the Lord.

4. This is the purpose of God in creation:
   all shall be changed for the Gospel is true –
   sickness to health, apathy to believing,
   doubt to commitment and old into new.

JLB

81   *Dismay & Distress / Faith / Lent & Passiontide*
Southwell 6686 (SM)

THOUGH HOPE DESERT MY HEART

1. Though hope desert my heart,
   though strangeness fill my soul,
   though truth torment my troubled mind,
   you have been here before.

2. Though confidence run dry,
   though weary flesh be sore,
   though conversation bear no fruit,
   you have been here before.

3. There is no threatening place,
   no trial I could know
   which has not known your presence first:
   you have been here before.

4. In Christ who, on the cross,
   felt all our hurt and more,
   and cried in deep abandonment,
   you have been here before.

5. I will not dread the dark,
   the fate beyond control,
   nor fear what reigns in frightening things;
   you will be there before.

This text is appropriate for use on Holy Saturday

JLB

82   *Holy Scripture / Saints of God*
Ellacombe 8686D (DCM)

THROUGH ABRAHAM AND MOSES

1. Through Abraham and Moses,
   through Deborah and Ruth,
   through Amos and Isaiah,
   God uttered holy truth.
   Each, with their own experience
   and knowledge of their Lord,
   contributed as witness to,
   and bearer of God's word.

2. While David's gift was poetry,
   and Miriam's gift was song,
   St John supplied a vision
   of right defeating wrong.
   Through stories, laws and letters,
   the pen outdid the sword
   and anchored all in Jesus Christ,
   true author of God's word.

3. So we revere the scriptures,
   both worldly and sublime,
   which none will fully comprehend
   this side of heaven and time.
   We honour all whose passion
   has been and is outpoured
   in mining old and new delights
   embodied in God's Word.

4. But more than that we honour God
   who gave us eyes to see
   the Word made flesh, and ears to hear
   the truth that sets us free.
   Through honest study, praise and prayer
   we grasp the golden cord
   that links the Gospel and our lives
   to Jesus Christ our Lord.

JLB

WE CANNOT MEASURE

1. We cannot measure how you heal
   or answer every sufferer's prayer;
   yet we believe your love responds
   when faith and doubt unite to care.
   Your hands, though bloodied on the cross,
   survive to hold and heal and warn,
   to carry all through death to life
   and cradle children yet unborn.

2. The pain that will not go away,
   the guilt that clings from things long past,
   the fear of what the future holds
   are present as if meant to last.
   But present too is love which tends
   the hurt we never hoped to find,
   the private agonies inside,
   the memories that haunt the mind.

3. So some have come who need your help,
   and some have come to make amends
   as hands, which shaped and saved the world,
   are present in the touch of friends.
   Lord, let your Spirit meet us here
   to mend the body, mind and soul,
   to disentangle peace from pain,
   and make your broken people whole.

84 *Marriage*
Repton 86 88 66

WE COME, DEAR GOD, TO CELEBRATE

1. We come, dear God, to celebrate
   the love our friends have found;
   and thank you, God, for their embrace,
   the joy and promise in this place
   which makes it holy ground,
   which makes it holy ground.

2. Help them fulfil the vows made here;
   let this new family share
   a welcome home, a future blessed
   by love and laughter, grace and guest
   with time enough to spare
   and kindness everywhere.

3. In seeking what the future holds,
   in letting go the past,
   prepare them both to clear a way
   through what must go and what should stay
   since love is meant to last,
   since love is meant to last.

JLB

85   *Death & Bereavement*
Rowan Tree / Resignation   8686 D (DCM)

WE DID NOT KNOW

1. We did not know what life was like
   before our birthing day;
   nor could we tell what we might do
   become, believe or say.
   Each life emerges as a gift,
   unique by heaven's design.
   So thank God for the mystery
   through which our lives combine.

2. And thank God for the travelled road
   which brought us to this day,
   for all we've gone through, all that's past,
   and all that's meant to stay;
   for those who shared the light of love
   and quietly showed their care,
   and those who recognised in us
   more than we thought was there.

3. We never know what each day holds:
   what need will be expressed,
   what deep desire will be fulfilled,
   what grief will be our guest.
   God did not guarantee us life
   untouched by death or pain,
   but promised all can work for good
   while life and love remain.

4. Oh Jesus, who shed tears of grief
   when you, too, lost a friend,
   be close to us who can but hope
   for life beyond life's end.
   Embrace the one we've loved and lost
   as fondly as we would;
   call *her** by name and keep *her** now   *(or *him*)
   both safe and understood.

JLB

86   *Abuse / Illness & Healing*
Horsley / St Columba   8686 (CM)

WE DO NOT ASK

1. We do not ask that heaven research
   the causes of our need;
   we yearn to know that when we pray
   God listens and takes heed.

2. We do not ask to be exempt
   from grief or guilt or pain;
   we deeply hope that suffering
   is not endured in vain.

3. For some face death or fear the dark,
   some fret for what might be;
   and some, too ill to name their plight,
   still plead to be set free.

4. And some, in body or in mind
   bear scars that mark their past,
   and long that stigmas be removed
   and truth be told at last.

5. Companion us, Lord Jesus Christ,
   to witness our distress.
   In solidarity and love
   forgive, restore and bless.

JLB

87

Discipleship / God's Grace / Joy
Lewis Air / Nettleton 8787 D

WE REJOICE TO BE GOD'S CHOSEN

1. We rejoice to be God's chosen
   not through virtue, work or skill,
   but because God's love is generous,
   unconformed to human will.
   And because God's love is restless
   like the surging of the sea,
   we are pulled by heaven's dynamic
   to become, not just to be.

2. We rejoice to be God's chosen,
   to be gathered to God's side
   not to build a pious ghetto
   or be steeped in selfish pride,
   but to celebrate the goodness
   of the one who sets us free
   from the smallness of our vision
   to become, not just to be.

3. We rejoice to be God's chosen,
   to align with heaven's intent,
   to await where we are summoned
   and accept where we are sent.
   We rejoice to be God's chosen
   and, amidst all that we see,
   to anticipate with wonder
   that the best is yet to be.

JLB

88 *Abuse*
Wer Nur Den Lieben Gott (Neumark) 98 98 88

FOR THOSE WHOSE SONG IS SILENT

1. We sing for those whose song is silent,
   whose hidden hurt no tune could bear –
   children whose innocence of loving
   has long since gone beyond repair.
   God, who conceived and gave us birth,
   listen for those who've lost their worth.

2. We sing for those who lives were mangled
   when friendship turned to vile abuse,
   as those they trusted traded kindness
   for cruelty beyond excuse.
   God, in whose image all were made,
   feel for the ones who've been betrayed.

3. We sing for those who bear within them
   scars in the body, mind and soul,
   fears from the past and, for tomorrow,
   yearnings that they might yet be whole.
   God, who in Christ was touched by pain,
   make your hurt children whole again.

4. We pray for those who know temptation
   worse than our earnest words can tell,
   who covet power, who lie in waiting
   with evil lusts designed in hell.
   Jesus, through whom the world is saved,
   conquer the sin, heal the depraved.

5. We sing that through believing people
   lives may be hallowed as they should;
   and ask that God in every victim
   shall see faith, hope and love renewed.
   This is our prayer, this is our song
   to God, to whom we all belong.

JLB

89   *Holy Communion*
Chartres / Hyfrydol 8787 D

THE HAND OF HEAVEN

1. We, who live by sound and symbol,
   we, who learn from sight and word,
   find these married in the person
   of the one we call our Lord.
   Taking bread to be his body,
   taking wine to be his blood,
   he let thought take flesh in action,
   he let faith take root in food.

2. Not just once with special people,
   not just hidden deep in time,
   but wherever Christ is followed,
   earthly fare becomes sublime.
   Though to sound this seems a mystery,
   though to sense it seems absurd,
   yet in faith, which seems like folly,
   we meet Jesus Christ our Lord.

3. God our Maker, send your Spirit
   to pervade the bread we break.
   Let it bring the life we long for
   and the love which we forsake.
   Bind us closer to each other,
   both forgiving and forgiven;
   give us grace in this and all things
   to discern the hand of heaven.

JLB & GM

90   *Discipleship / Jesus' Life & Ministry / Lent & Passiontide*
                                     O Waly, Waly   8888 (LM)

GOD ON EARTH

1. When God Almighty came to earth,
   he took the pain of Jesus' birth;
   he took the flight of refugee
   and whispered, 'Humbly follow me.'

2. When God Almighty went to work,
   carpenter's sweat he did not shirk;
   profit and loss he did not flee,
   but whispered, 'Humbly follow me.'

3. When God Almighty walked the street,
   the critic's curse he had to meet;
   the cynic's smile he had to see
   and whispered, 'Humbly follow me.'

4. When God Almighty met his folk,
   of peace and truth he gladly spoke
   to set the slave and tyrant free,
   and whispered, 'Humbly follow me.'

5. When God Almighty took his place
   to save the fallen human race
   he took it boldly on a tree
   and whispered, 'Humbly follow me.'

6. When God Almighty comes again
   he'll meet us incognito as then;
   and though no words may voice his plea,
   he'll whisper, 'Are you following me?'

JLB & GM

WHEN GOD CREATED HUMANKIND

1. When God created humankind
   diversity was kept in mind;
   thus race and culture helped proclaim
   that none were meant to be the same.

2. To underscore that this was meant,
   a sign was made of heaven's intent:
   God's image in each mortal ran
   as much in woman as in man.

3. And thus acknowledged was the fact
   that differences can yet attract,
   and be the very means through which
   we counterbalance and enrich.

4. That all may grow and change and move,
   God gave the gift of holy love,
   intended to fulfil and bind
   commitments made by heart and mind.

5. So let us celebrate and praise
   the skill and will of God always;
   and on this happy day rejoice
   as two we love confirm their choice.

JLB

92 — Advent / Christmas
Columcille / Normandy 6565 D

WHEN JOSEPH WAS BRIDEGROOM

1. When Joseph was bridegroom and Mary the bride,
   the date of their wedding was his to decide,
   for Mary was pregnant and Joseph beguiled
   till Gabriel convinced him to parent God's child.

2. So, Joseph consented to take second place
   and save his beloved from certain disgrace;
   informed by what Mary proclaimed in her song,
   he kept faith though fearing that much might go wrong.

3. In touch with an angel, inspired by a dream,
   aware that things sometimes are more than they seem,
   confronted by God in sound, silence and sight,
   all Joseph desired was to do what was right.

4. O God, who called Joseph to father your son,
   and see, as a tradesman, your will being done,
   teach us, when reluctant to stay on your side
   like Joseph, though doubting, to dream then decide.

JLB

93   Holy Spirit / Jesus' Life & Ministry / Pentecost
Personent Hodie   666 66 and refrain

GIFTS OF THE SPIRIT

1. When our Lord walked the earth,
   all the world found its worth;
   as declared at his birth,
   God became our neighbour,
   granting us with favour

   > *Chorus:*
   > POWER TO SPEAK AND HEAL,
   > GRACE TO KNOW WHAT'S REAL,
   > WISDOM, INSIGHT AND FAITH,
   > LOVE AND UNDERSTANDING.

2. Through his life, through his death,
   in each gesture and breath,
   Jesus joined faith and deed,
   model for our caring,
   showing and yet sharing

3. Jesus loves all his friends,
   and that love never ends;
   to his Church gifts he sends
   through the Holy Spirit.
   These we still inherit:

4. Sing and smile and rejoice,
   clap your hands, raise your voice;
   for, with unnerving choice,
   God in Christ has found us
   and displays around us

JLB & GM

THE TRUTH THAT SETS US FREE

1. When the wheel of fate is turning
   and the mills of God grind slow,
   when the past seems more attractive
   than the future we don't know,
   when our confidence is waning
   and we lack security,
   comes the timeless word of Jesus
   that the truth will set us free.

2. Is it war or economics,
   is it danger or deceit,
   is it unforeseen depression,
   fear of failure to compete?
   Have the times which once were changing
   led where no one wants to be?
   Shall we live by lies on offer
   or the truth that sets us free?

3. With real faith there will be doubting,
   and with loss there will be grief.
   No one knows the contradictions
   which will exercise belief.
   Against conflicts life might bring us,
   God provides no guarantee,
   just this word of hope and healing:
   know that truth will set you free.

4. So, dear Jesus, make us willing
   to unmask convenient lies,
   to protest wherever power
   closes conscience, ears and eyes;
   and release our expectations
   of your kingdom yet to be,
   born in courage, joy and justice
   and the truth that sets us free.

JLB

95   *Easter / Jesus' Life and Ministry*
                                    Sussex Carol   88 88 88

TORN IN TWO

1. Where sight and insight lose their way,
   we segregate familiar ground
   from where we think you ought to stay
   and peace and paradise abound:
   In Christ you tore the barrier down –
   the Word made flesh let heaven be known.

2. When Holy Grace took human form
   and called earth's outcast folk his friends,
   when Heaven's Original revealed
   the path required to make amends,
   we felt compelled to fret and fuss.
   You know – for you were here with us.

3. In warm embrace for withered arms,
   in dining out with tarnished guests,
   in breaking umpteen petty rules,
   in controversial, quiet requests,
   barriers dividing heaven from earth
   were bulldozed to reveal our worth.

4. Still we are hesitant to see
   that all of life is yours to save,
   that peace and politics and power
   adorn your birthplace and your grave,
   that rising you redeemed the fraud
   of virtue trying to shelter God.

5. Ah, Holy Jesus, come again
   wherever we would keep you out.
   Destroy our sanctimonious shrouds
   and demonstrate to all who doubt:
   the temple's veil is torn in two
   and all of life is sacred now.

JLB & GM

96

Christmas
Beach Spring / Hyfrydol 8787 D

GOD'S SURPRISE

1. Who would think that what was needed
   to transform and save the earth
   might not be a plan or army,
   proud in purpose, proved in worth?
   Who would think, despite derision,
   that a child might lead the way?
   God surprises earth with heaven,
   coming here on Christmas Day.

2. Shepherds watch and wise men wonder,
   monarchs scorn and angels sing;
   such a place as none could reckon
   hosts a holy, helpless thing.
   Stable beasts and bypassed strangers
   watch a baby laid in hay;
   God surprises earth with heaven
   coming here on Christmas Day.

3. Centuries of skill and science
   span the past from which we move,
   yet experience questions whether,
   with such progress, we improve.
   While the human lot we ponder,
   lest our hopes and humour fray,
   God surprises earth with heaven
   coming here on Christmas Day.

JLB & GM

97   Confirmation / Discipleship
Kelvingrove   76 76 77 76

THE SUMMONS

1. 'Will you come and follow me
   if I but call your name?
   Will you go where you don't know
   and never be the same?
   Will you let my love be shown,
   will you let my name be known,
   will you let my life be grown
   in you and you in me?'

2. 'Will you leave yourself behind
   if I but call your name?
   Will you care for cruel and kind
   and never be the same?
   Will you risk the hostile stare
   should your life attract or scare?
   Will you let me answer prayer
   in you and you in me?'

3. 'Will you let the blinded see
   if I but call your name?
   Will you set the prisoners free
   and never be the same?
   Will you kiss the leper clean
   and do such as this unseen,
   and admit to what I mean
   in you and you in me?'

4. 'Will you love the 'you' you hide
   if I but call your name?
   Will you quell the fear inside
   and never be the same?
   Will you use the faith you've found
   to reshape the world around
   through my sight and touch and sound
   in you and you in me?'

(over)

JLB & GM

5. Lord, your summons echoes true
   when you but call my name.
   Let me turn and follow you
   and never be the same.
   In your company I'll go
   where your love and footsteps show.
   Thus I'll move and live and grow
   in you and you in me.

98

Creation
Brother James' Air / Land Of Rest 8686 (CM)

WITH GRACE AND CAREFULNESS

1. With grace and carefulness, O Lord,
   you tend as you designed;
   your providence prepares the earth
   to prosper humankind. *

2. You water furrows, level hills,
   and soften ground with showers;
   with kindly gifts you crown the year,
   good growth your grace empowers. *

3. Wherever harvest fields are ripe
   your tracks can be perceived;
   the desert lands turn verdant green,
   the hills with joy are wreathed. *

4. The meadows clothe themselves with sheep
   and valleys drip with grain;
   they sing your praise, then shout aloud
   and praise your name again. *

   When sung to Brother James' Air, repeat the last two lines of each verse.

   Paraphrase of Psalm 65: 9-13

JLB

99   *Confirmation / Holy Communion*
Repton 86 88 66

WITHIN THE CIRCLE OF YOUR FRIENDS

1. Within the circle of your friends,
   you found a place for me.
   Beside those whom I often meet,
   near people whom I've yet to greet
   I'm privileged to be,
   I'm privileged to be.

2. Within your commonwealth of love,
   you found a place for me
   to listen, heal, disturb or care,
   seek words to sing, find truth to share,
   let life be full and free,
   let life be full and free.

3. Around the table you prepare,
   you found a place for me
   where, breaking bread and pouring wine,
   you tell us all, 'This means you're mine.
   and mine you'll always be,
   and mine you'll always be.'

4. Now brother, servant, saviour, Lord,
   I make a place for you.
   Called to your feast, among your friends,
   and keen to live as God intends,
   I come to be made new,
   I come to be made new.

JLB

Civic Life & Social Justice / Human Life / Penitence
Kom Nu Met Zang   98 98 966

WOMEN AND MEN AS GOD INTENDED

1. Women and men as God intended,
   daughters of Adam, sons of Eve;
   children of earth, loved by their Maker,
   those only heaven could conceive;
   yet in our loving we are not one
   with heaven's deep intent:
   we are not as God meant.

2. Ours is the shame, ours is the story,
   ours is the squandered legacy;
   fallen from grace, fearful of glory,
   lost is our true humanity.
   How can the goodness heaven endowed,
   which earth cannot afford
   be once again restored?

3. Into our world, born of a woman,
   comes, in the flesh, the living God,
   moved by our plight, suffering rejection,
   feeling for those whose lives are flawed.
   Pardoning all who truly repent
   comes Jesus Christ our Lord,
   God's liberating Word.

4. Now sing aloud! Jesus our brother
   turns every tide of history,
   sharing our flesh, bearing our sorrow,
   winning an endless liberty.
   Out of the grave, alive in the world,
   Christ wills all be made new:
   this tested Word is true.

JLB

COPYRIGHT

The texts in this collection are by John L. Bell & Graham Maule and are copyright:

© WGRG, c/o Iona Community, Glasgow, Scotland.
www.wildgoose.scot

and are secured for congregatonal use under the CCL and Decani (Calamus) licensing schemes, in territories where these licences apply.

For other territories and for commercial reproduction, permission should be sought from:

Wild Goose Resource Group / WGRG
c/o The Iona Community
21 Carlton Court,
GLASGOW G5 9JP

wildgoose@wildgoose.scot
www.wildgoose.scot

ALPHABETICAL INDEX OF FIRST LINES

Note: * indicates a previously unpublished text

	First line of Text	Tune (and alternative)
1.*	Aged ninety and a hundred years	KINGSFOLD
2.	Ageless God of boundless wonder	HOLY MANNA
3.	All the wonder that surrounds us	AR HYD Y NOS
4.*	All who throng the halls of heaven	EBENEZER
5.	Among us and before us, Lord, you stand	SURSUM CORDA
6.*	And did you know that on the very night	EVENTIDE
7.	As we walked home at close of day	CONDITOR ALME / EISENACH
8.	Because the Saviour prayed, 'May they be one'	WOODLANDS
9.*	Because you had an upstairs room prepared	SURSUM CORDA
10.	Bless, O my soul, bless God the Lord	RICHMOND
11.	Christ has risen while earth slumbers	BLAENWERN / HYFRYDOL
12.	Come, host of heaven's high dwelling place	ST COLUMBA
13.	Conceiver of both heaven and earth	O WALY WALY
14.	Do not be vexed or envy	COLESHILL / ST ANNE
15.	For all the saints who showed your love	TALLIS CANON / O WALY WALY
16.*	For each time there is a season	BEACH SPRING
17.*	From Adam came the apple	ELLACOMBE
18.	From heaven's attendant host you came	WINCHESTER NEW
19.	Give us, this year, an adult Christmas	NEUMARK
20.	Go, silent friend, your life has found its ending	LONDONDERRY AIR
21.*	God and parent of all people	HYFRYDOL / CHARTRES
22.	God beyond glory	SCHÖNSTER HERR JESU
23.	God, give us life	LAND OF REST / GERONTIUS
24.	God it was who said to Abram	HOLY MANNA / LEWIS AIR
25.*	God loved the world so much	WONDROUS LOVE

Alphabetical Index of First Lines

26.	God our creator	BUNESSAN
27.*	God's is a world of beauty	THORNBURY
28.	God's Spirit came at Pentecost	SUSSEX CAROL
29.	God's spirit is here	HANOVER / LAUDATE DOMINUM
30.*	Help us accept the past	LOVE UNKNOWN
31.	How can we stand together	SEVEN JOYS OF MARY
32.	I come in faith and fear to God	AN COINEACHAN (HIGHLAND FAIRY LULLABY)
33.	I love the Lord because he heard	MARTYRDOM / LAND OF REST
34.	I owe my Lord a morning song	BROTHER JAMES' AIR
35.	I sit outside the rich world's gate	KINGSFOLD
36.	I waited patiently for God	NEW BRITAIN
37.	Inspired by love and anger	SALLEY GARDENS
38.	Is God who made and loves the world	GONFALON ROYAL / AGINCOURT
39.	Jesus calls us here to meet him	LEWIS AIR / BLAENWERN
40.	Jesus Christ is risen	NOEL NOUVELET
41.	Jesus Christ is waiting	NOEL NOUVELET
42.*	Jesus was doubted when he said	O WALY, WALY / SUANTRAI
43.	Just as a lost and thirsty deer	HESPERUS / O WALY, WALY
44.	Keep me Lord, for in your keeping	HYFRYDOL
45.*	Let every nation on the earth	DUKE STREET / TALLIS CANON
46.*	Long have you loved me, Holy God	DOMINUS REGIT ME / ST COLUMBA
47.	Lord Jesus Christ, shall I stand still	YE BANKS AND BRAES
48.*	Lord, when your kingdom comes	EVENTIDE
49.*	Monarch and maker of all time and space	WOODLANDS
50.	No wind at the window	COLUMCILLE

Alphabetical Index of First Lines

51.	Not the powerful, not the privileged	GOTT WILL'S MACHEN
52.*	Not through merit, not through skill	LIEBSTER JESU
53.	O Christ, you wept when grief was raw	ROCKINGHAM
54.	O God, with holy righteousness	FOREST GREEN
55.	O God, you are my God alone	RESIGNATION / COE FEN
56.	O Lord our Lord, throughout the earth	ELLACOMBE
57.*	Of all that we enjoy in harmony with heaven	LOVE UNKNOWN
58.	Oh where are you going?	STREETS OF LAREDO
59.	Out of the direst depths	SOUTHWELL
60.	Praise the Lord, the ground of goodness	LAUS DEO / STUTTGART
61.	Praise to the Lord for the joys of the earth	SLANE
62.	Praise with joy the world's creator	LAUDA ANIMA (PRAISE, MY SOUL)
63.*	Shout for joy, you sons and daughters	BLAENWERN / ODE TO JOY
64.	Sing, my soul, when hope is sleeping	GOTT WILL'S MACHEN
65.	Sing praise to God on mountain tops	VICAR OF BRAY / HOW CAN I KEEP FROM SINGING?
66.	Sing to God with joy and gladness	ALL FOR JESUS / STUTTGART
67.	Sisters and brothers, with one voice	VULPIUS
68.*	The day soon will come	LOCH LOMOND
69.	The God of all eternity	WINCHESTER NEW
70.*	The hope that hides in Bethlehem	EISENACH / VERBUM SUPERNUM
71.*	The house of God is our delight	TALLIS CANON
72.	The love of God comes close	LOVE UNKNOWN
73.*	The 'other person' Jesus saw	MARTYRDOM / NEW BRITAIN
74.*	The soldiers fear the captain's wrath	NOEL
75.*	The time has come when from the past	SUSSEX CAROL
76.*	The whole creation waits	SOUTHWELL
77.*	The word of God is like a lamp	LAND OF REST /

Alphabetical Index of First Lines

78. There is a line of women	ST COLUMBA / SEVEN JOYS OF MARY
79.* There travelled Joseph and his bride	FOREST GREEN
80.* This is God's house	WAS LEBET, WAS SCHWEBET
81.* Though hope desert my heart	SOUTHWELL
82.* Through Abraham and Moses	ELLACOMBE
83. We cannot measure how you heal	YE BANKS AND BRAES
84.* We come, dear Lord, to celebrate	REPTON
85.* We did not know what life was like	ROWAN TREE / RESIGNATION
86.* We do not ask that heaven research	HORSLEY / ST. COLUMBA
87. We rejoice to be God's chosen	NETTLETON / LEWIS AIR
88.* We sing for those whose song is silent	WER NUR DEN LIEBEN GOTT (NEUMARK)
89. We who live by sound and symbol	CHARTRES / HYFRYDOL
90. When God Almighty came to earth	O WALY, WALY
91.* When God created humankind	PUER NOBIS NASCITUR
92.* When Joseph was bridegroom	COLUMCILLE / NORMANDY
93. When our Lord walked the earth	PERSONENT HODIE
94. When the wheel of fate is turning	CHARTRES / EBENEZER
95. Where sight and insight lose their way	SUSSEX CAROL
96. Who would think that what was needed	BEACH SPRING / HYFRYDOL
97. Will you come and follow me	KELVINGROVE
98. With grace and carefulness	BROTHER JAMES' AIR / LAND OF REST
99.* Within the circle of your friends	REPTON
100. Women and men as God intended	KOM NU MET ZANG

COMMON TUNES & THEIR METRES

Tune	Metre	Song.No.
AGINCOURT	8888 (LM)	38
ALL FOR JESUS	8787	66
AN COINEACHAN (HIGHLAND FAIRY LULLABY)		
	8887 & Chorus	32
AR HYD Y NOS	8484 8884	3
BEACH SPRING	8787 D	16, 96
BLAENWERN	8787 D	11, 39, 63
BROTHER JAMES' AIR	8686 (CM)	34, 98
BUNESSAN	5554 D	26
CHARTRES	8787 D	21, 89, 94
COE FEN	8686 D (DCM)	55
COLESHILL	8686 (CM)	14
COLUMCILLE	6565 D	50, 92
CONDITOR ALME	8888 (LM)	7
DOMINUS REGIT ME	8787	46
DUKE STREET	8888 (LM)	45
EBENEZER	8787 D	4, 94
EISENACH	8888 (LM)	7, 70
ELLACOMBE	8686 D	17, 56, 82
EVENTIDE	10 10 10 10	6, 48
FOREST GREEN	8686 D (DCM)	54, 79
GAELIC LULLABY	8887 & Refrain	32
GERONTIUS	8686 (CM)	23
GONFALON ROYAL	8888 (LM)	38, 91
GOTT WILL'S MACHEN	8787	51, 64
HANOVER	10 10 11 11	29
HESPERUS	8888 (LM)	43
HIGHLAND CATHEDRAL	10 10 10 10	49
HOLY MANNA	8787 D	2, 24
HORSLEY	8686 (CM)	86
HOW CAN I KEEP FROM SINGING?		
	8787 D	65
HYFRYDOL	8787 D	11, 21, 44, 89, 96

Common Tunes & Their Metres

Tune	Metre	Song.No.
KELVINGROVE	7676 7776	97
KINGSFOLD	8686 D (DCM)	1, 35
KOM NU MET ZANG	98 98 966	100
LAND OF REST	8686 (CM)	23, 33, 77, 98
LAUDA ANIMA (PRAISE, MY SOUL)	878787	62
LAUDATE DOMINUM	10 10 11 11	29
LAUS DEO	8787	60
LEWIS AIR	8787 D	24, 39, 87
LIEBESTER JESU	7878 88	52
LOCH LOMOND	11 9 11 9 D	68
LONDONDERRY AIR	11 10 11 10	20
LOVE UNKNOWN	66 66 88	30, 57, 72
MARTYRDOM (FENWICK)	8686 (CM)	33, 73
NEW BRITAIN (AMAZING GRACE)	8686 (CM)	36, 73
NETTLETON	8787 D	87
NOEL	8686 D (DCM)	74
NOEL NOUVELET	11 11 10 11	40, 41
NORMANDY	6565 D	92
O WALY, WALY	8888 (LM)	13, 15, 42, 43, 90
ODE TO JOY	8787 D	63
PERSONENT HODIE	Irregular	93
PUER NOBIS NASCITUR	8888 (LM)	91
REPTON	86 88 66	84, 99
RESIGNATION	8686 D (DCM)	55, 85
RICHMOND	8686 (CM)	10
ROCKINGHAM	8888 (LM)	53
ROWAN TREE	8686 D (DCM)	85
ST ANNE	8686 (CM)	14
ST COLUMBA	8686 (CM)	12, 46, 77, 86
SALLEY GARDENS	7676 D	37
SCHÖNSTER HERR JESU	559 558	22
SEVEN JOYS OF MARY	8686 D (DCM)	31, 78
SLANE	10 10 10 10	61

Common Tunes & Their Metres

Tune	Metre	Song.No.
SOUTHWELL	6686 (SM)	59, 76, 81
STUTTGART	8787	60, 66
STREETS OF LAREDO	6665 D	58
SUANTRAI	8888 (LM)	42
SURSUM CORDA	10 10 10 10	5, 9
SUSSEX CAROL	88 88 88	28, 75, 95
TALLIS CANON	8888 (LM)	15, 45, 71
THORNBURY	7676 D	27
VERBUM SUPERNUM	8888 (LM)	70
VICAR OF BRAY	8787 D	65
VULPIUS	888 & Refrain	67
WAS LEBET, WAS SCHWEBET	11 10 11 10	80
WER NUR DEN LIEBEN GOTT (NEUMARK) 98 98 88		19, 88
WINCHESTER NEW	8888 (LM)	18, 69
WOODLANDS	10 10 10 10	8, 49
WONDROUS LOVE	Irregular	25
YE BANKS AND BRAES	8888 D (DLM)	47, 83

PSALMS IN PARAPHRASE

Psalm	First Line	Song No.
8	O Lord, our Lord, throughout the earth	56
16	Keep me, Lord, for in your keeping	44
29	All who throng the halls of heaven	4
33	Shout for joy, you sons and daughters	63
37	Do not be vexed or envy those	14
40	I waited patiently for God	36
42	Just as a lost and thirsty deer	43
63	O God, you are my God alone	55
65	With grace and carefulness	98
72	O God, with holy righteousness	54
100	Let every nation on the earth	45
103	Bless, O My Soul, the Lord your God	10
116	I love the Lord, because he heard	33
130	Out of the direst depths	59
147	Sing for joy	66

SUBJECTS & THEMES

Subject	Song. No.
Abuse	74, 86, 88
Advent	19, 50, 54, 68, 70, 75, 79, 92
Baptism	13, 21
Change	42, 69
Christian Unity	8, 28, 66
Christmas	19, 51, 70, 74, 92, 96
Church	12, 18, 28, 71, 80
Civic Life & Social Justice	14, 31, 35, 37, 38, 60, 68, 100
Commitment	24, 26, 32, 47, 67
Confirmation	18, 25, 26 32, 47, 67, 97, 99
Creation	2, 3, 4, 27, 49, 56, 65, 66, 76, 98
Death & Bereavement	20, 23, 53, 64, 76, 85,
Discipleship	25, 29, 37, 39, 41, 46, 58, 67, 87, 90, 97
Dismay & Distress	14, 43, 59, 64, 81, 83, 94
Easter	7, 11, 40, 42, 95
Faith	33, 36, 44, 52, 55, 73, 81
God's Grace	3, 10, 33, 36, 44, 46, 52, 73, 87
God's Majesty	4, 54
Holy Communion	5, 6, 9, 32, 33, 39, 52, 72, 89, 99
Holy Scripture	1, 17, 24, 74, 77, 78, 82
Holy Spirit	12, 28, 29, 93
Holy Trinity	26, 34, 62
Human Life	17, 27, 30, 57, 61, 100
Illness & Healing	23, 43, 64, 83, 86
Interfaith Issues	38, 66
Jesus' Life & Ministry	5, 17, 25, 31, 35, 37, 38, 41, 53, 58, 90, 93, 95
Joy	1, 44, 72, 87
Lent & Passiontide	6, 9, 33, 47, 48, 81, 90
Life After Death	30
Love	46, 57, 72
Marriage	16, 22, 57, 84, 91
New Year	69

Subjects & Themes

Subject	Song. No.
Peace	75
Penitence	30, 32, 48, 59, 100
Pentecost	28, 29, 93
Praise Of God	4, 10, 34, 45, 56, 60, 61, 62, 63, 65, 66, 86
Saints Of God	1, 15, 24, 78, 82
Truth	2, 63, 94
Women	78
Worship	12, 26, 39, 71, 80

THE WILD GOOSE RESOURCE GROUP

The Wild Goose Resource Group is a semi-autonomous project of the Iona Community, committed to the renewal of public worship. Based in Glasgow, the WGRG has three resource workers, John Bell, Jo Love and Graham Maule, who lead workshops, seminars and events throughout Britain and abroad. They are supported by Gail Ullrich, who fulfils the role of the Group's administrator.

The task of the WGRG has been to develop and identify new methods and materials to enable the revitalisation of congregational song, prayer and liturgy. Songs and liturgical material have been translated and used in many countries across the world as well as being frequently broadcast on radio and television. From time to time, the Wild Goose Collective – an ad hoc assortment of singers associated with the Group – record new songs by WGRG.

The WGRG, along with the Iona Community Programme Team, run weeWONDERBOX, a programme of ecumenical workshop and worship events, mainly at the Iona Community's Base in the centre of Glasgow, though occasionally also further afield.

The WGRG also publish a Liturgy Booklet series as well as a newsletter, *GOOSEgander*, to enable friends and supporters to keep up to date with WGRG developments.

If you would like to find out more about subscribing to these, or about ways to support the WGRG financially, please contact:

Wild Goose Resource Group,
c/o Iona Community,
21 Carlton Court,
Glasgow G5 9JP, Scotland.

Tel: 0141 429 7281
E-mail: wildgoose@wildgoose.scot
Web: www.wildgoose.scot
Twitter: WildGooseRG
Facebook: Wild Goose Resource Group

WILD GOOSE RESOURCE GROUP TITLES

SONGBOOKS, & CDs

Come All You People, John L. Bell / Wild Goose Worship Group. Book: ISBN 9780947988685 / CD: 9781901557404.
Courage To Say No, The, John L. Bell & Graham Maule / Wild Goose Worship Group. Book: ISBN 9780947988784; CD: ISBN 9781901557442.
Enemy Of Apathy, John L. Bell & Graham Maule / Wild Goose Collective. Book: ISBN 9780947988272.
Heaven Shall Not Wait, John L. Bell & Graham Maule / Wild Goose Worship Group. Book: ISBN 9781901557800; CD ISBN 9781901557459.
I Will Not Sing Alone, John L. Bell / Wild Goose Collective. Book: 9781901557916; CD: ISBN 9781901557893.
Innkeepers & Light Sleepers, John L. Bell / Wild Goose Worship Group. Book: ISBN 9780947988470; CD: ISBN 9781901557398.
Love & Anger, John L. Bell & Graham Maule / Wild Goose Worship Group. Book: ISBN 9780947988982; CD: ISBN 9781901557411.
Love From Below, John L. Bell & Graham Maule / Wild Goose Worship Group. Book: ISBN 0 947988 34 3; CD: ISBN 9781901557466.
One Is The Body, John L. Bell / Wild Goose Worship Group. Book: ISBN 9781901557350; CD: ISBN 9781901557374.
Psalms Of Patience, Protest & Praise, John L. Bell / Wild Goose Worship Group. Book: ISBN 9780947988562; CD: ISBN 9780947988579.
There Is One Among Us, John L. Bell / Wild Goose Worship Group. Book: ISBN 9781901557107; CD: 9781901557213.
Truth That Sets Us Free, The, John L. Bell / Wild Goose Collective. Book: ISBN 9781849522304; CD: ISBN 9781849522403.
We Walk His Way, John L. Bell / Wild Goose Collective. Book: ISBN 9781905010554; CD: ISBN 9781905010424.
When Grief is Raw, John L. Bell & Graham Maule. Book: ISBN 9780947988913.

CHORAL ANTHEM PACKS & CDs

God Comes Tomorrow, John L. Bell & The Cathedral Singers. Anthem Pack: GIA G-4376; CD: GIA CD-494.

Wild Goose Resource Group Titles

God Never Sleeps, John L. Bell & The Cathedral Singers. Anthem Pack: GIA G-4376; CD: GIA CD-348.
Last Journey, The, John L. Bell & The Cathedral Singers. Book: GIA G-4527P; Anthem Pack: GIA G-4527; CD: GIA CD-381.
Seven Psalms Of David, John L. Bell. Anthem Pack: GIA G-4830.
Seven Songs Of Mary, John L. Bell. Book: GIA G-4652.
Psalms Of David, Songs Of Mary, John L. Bell & The Cathedral Singers. CD: GIA CD-403
Splendour Of The House Of God, The, John L. Bell. & The Cathedral Singers. Anthem Pack: GIA G-8099; CD: GIA CD-874.
Take This Moment, John L. Bell & The Cathedral Singers. Anthem Pack: GIA G-5155; CD: GIA CD-464.

SONG METHODOLOGY

Singing Thing, The – A case for congregational song, John L. Bell. Book: ISBN 9781901557282.
Singing Thing Too, The – Enabling congregations to sing, John L. Bell. Book: ISBN 9781905010325.

RESOURCE BOOKS

Cloth For The Cradle – Advent, Christmas & Epiphany, Wild Goose Worship Group. Book: ISBN 9781901557015.
He Was In The World – Meditations for public worship, John L Bell. Book: ISBN 9780947988708.
Jesus & Peter – Off-the-record conversations, John L. Bell & Graham Maule. Book: ISBN 9781901557176.
Present On Earth – The life of Jesus, Wild Goose Worship Group. Book: ISBN 9781901557640.
Stages On The Way – Lent, Holy Week & Easter, Wild Goose Worship Group. Book: ISBN 9781901557114
Wee Worship Book, A – 4th Incarnation, John L. Bell, Mairi Munro & WGRG. Book: ISBN 9781901557190.
Wee Worship Book, A – 5th Incarnation, John L. Bell & WGRG. Book: ISBN 9781849523226.

Wild Goose Resource Group Titles

THEOLOGICAL REFLECTIONS

10 Things They Never Told Me About Jesus – A beginner's guide to a larger Christ, John L. Bell. Book: ISBN 9781905010608.
All That Matters – Collected scripts from Radio 4's Thought for The Day, Vol.2, John L. Bell. Book: ISBN 9781849520706.
Hard Words For Interesting Times – Biblical texts in contemporary contexts, John L. Bell. Book: ISBN 9781901557756.
States Of Bliss & Yearning – The marks and means of authentic Christian spirituality, John L. Bell. Book: ISBN 9781901557077.
Thinking Out Loud – Collected scripts from Radio 4's Thought for The Day, Vol.1, John L. Bell. Book: ISBN 9781905010417.

WGRG LITURGY BOOKLETS

Spare Change & Gilt-Edged Grace – A liturgy exploring the relationship between faith and wealth, Wild Goose Resource Group. Liturgy Booklet no.12; ISBN 9781909469112.
God & Her Girls – A celebration of the giftedness of forgotten women, Wild Goose Resource Group. Liturgy Booklet no.11; ISBN 9781909469105.
Harvesting The World – A liturgy for harvest festivals, Wild Goose Resource Group. Liturgy Booklet no.10; ISBN 9781909469099.
Family Affair, A – A liturgy based on Jesus' most famous parable (the Prodigal Son), Wild Goose Resource Group. Liturgy Booklet no.9; ISBN 9781909469082.
Fencing In God's People – A liturgy on 3000 years of wall building in Israel & Palestine, Wild Goose Resource Group. Liturgy Booklet no.8; ISBN 9781909469075.
Road To Roam, A – A way of celebrating sacred space, Wild Goose Resource Group. Liturgy Booklet no.7; ISBN 9781909469068.
Sweet Honey & Hard Places – Prayer services based on the Psalms, Wild Goose Resource Group; Liturgy Booklet no.6; ISBN 9781909469051.
Pictures Of God – An act of worship about images, Wild Goose Resource Group. Liturgy Booklet no.5; ISBN 9781909469044.
Remember Me Today – A Holy Week reflection, Wild Goose Resource Group. Liturgy Booklet no.4; ISBN 9781909469037.

Wild Goose Resource Group Titles

Love Which Heals, The – A service of grieving & gratitude for those recently bereft, Wild Goose Resource Group. Liturgy Booklet no.3; ISBN 9781909469020.

Jubilee Liturgy, A – A liturgy for justice at the Millennium, Wild Goose Resource Group. Liturgy Booklet no.2; ISBN 9781909469013.

St Columba Of Iona – An order for the commemoration of the saint's life, Wild Goose Resource Group. Liturgy Booklet no.1; ISBN 9781909469006.

Order online at **www.wildgoose.scot** or **www.ionabooks.com**